NORTHWEST BOAT
DIVES
60

Ultimate Dives in
Puget Sound & Hood Canal

Dave Bliss

SASQUATCH BOOKS

SEATTLE

This book is dedicated to Rose and Sarah, who gave me a reason.
—D.B.

Printed in the United States of America.
Distributed in Canada by Raincoast Books Ltd.
01 00 99 98 97   5 4 3 2 1

Credits:
Cover design, interior design, and composition: Douglas Deay
Cover photograph: Fred Bavendam/ Tony Stone Images
Interior photographs: Dave Bliss, unless otherwise noted
Copy editor: Alice Copp Smith
Indexer: Justine Matthies

Library of Congress Cataloging in Publication Data
Bliss, Dave.
          Northwest boat dives : 60 ultimate dives in Puget Sound and Hood Canal / Dave Bliss.
                    p. cm.
          Includes bibliographical references and index.
          ISBN 1-57061-090-8
          1. Scuba diving—Washington (State)—Puget Sound Region—Guidebooks. 2. Scuba diving—
Washington (State)—Hood Canal—guidebooks. 3. Puget Sound Region (Wash.)—Guidebooks. 4. Hood
Canal Region (Wash.)—Guidebooks. I. Title.
GV838.673.U6B55   1997
797.2'3—dc21   96-50999

Sasquatch Books
615 Second Avenue
Seattle, Washington 98104
(206) 467-4300
books@sasquatchbooks.com
http://www.sasquatchbooks.com

Sasquatch Books publishes high-quality adult nonfiction and children's books related to the Northwest (Alaska to San Francisco). For more information about our titles, contact us at the address above, or view our site on the World Wide Web.

Contents

Acknowledgments

No work of this magnitude can be completed without the help and cooperation of many people. I would like to express a heartfelt thank you to the many divers who joined me, regardless of weather, in seeking quality dive sites throughout Puget Sound and Hood Canal, sometimes succeeding, sometimes failing, never complaining, always providing good information and assistance. Those divers include Chris Grote, Chip Jackson, Dan Fry, Amy Traner, Mike McIlwain, Steve Prade, T.J. Barcelona, and Carol Nottenburg. A very special thank you to Ed Buchwald for always being there, for his willingness to play any part, and for the inspiration he unknowingly provided.

Next, a debt of gratitude is owed to Dan and Laurie Berg and to Jim Bausano, for their help and hospitality and for an unforgettable day in Discovery Bay.

Thanks to Brett Green and Brian Brumbaugh for their support and the invaluable information and insight they provided regarding Puget Sound dive sites. Additionally, thank you to all of the dive shop owners, managers, and employees for their cooperation, assistance, and willingness to provide information or whatever services were needed to keep our act on the road. This group includes Orca Scuba Center, Sound Diver Center, Capital Divers, Underwater Sports, Puget Sound Dive Enterprises, Lighthouse Diving Center, Mikes Diving Center, Deep Fathom Diving Center, Whidbey Island Dive Center, Orca Divers, Lakewood Scuba, Hood Sport Dive Shop, and Langley Dive Shop, among others.

Thanks to Doug Melby for all the advice and input throughout the entire project and for assistance with photo equipment. Thanks to the Cooley family, Noel Siler, and the Narrows Marina staff for making room for us. Thanks to Jim White and Magellan Systems Corporation for assistance with a Global Positioning System and Differential Beacon Receiver.

Thanks to Eadie Montgomery, Cindy Steele, Sandy Peterson, and Zachary Williams for running our businesses so we could dedicate our time to this project, and to Michael and Patrick Stafford for their support and confidence.

I would like to thank Gary Luke of Sasquatch Books for his expertise and his support in this work.

A huge debt of gratitude is owed to David and Juanita Bliss for providing a motorhome for the entire duration of our research travels.

Finally, I wish to thank my wife and dive buddy, Rose Bliss, for being there everyday and doing far too many things to list; without her there would be no book. And my daughter Sarah, who makes it all worthwhile.

Prologue

We dive for many reasons. Some of us dive to hunt and collect. Others dive to take photographs. Some of us dive to go places we have never been and to see things we have never seen. Others of us dive simply because we like being surrounded by water. However, there is one thing that all recreational divers share in common: We dive because we love to dive, not because we have to.

Regardless of why we love to dive beneath the sea, we must remember we are privileged visitors to a fragile world. When a reef is damaged by a careless fin kick while we take photographs, the beauty of that spot, which overwhelmed us only moments before, may be gone for the rest of our lives. If we take all of the large fish from a reef, our hunting grounds become barren. If, instead of respecting the right to live that all creatures share, we capture octopuses and wolf eels, they will not be there to fill us with wonder on our next visit to the reef. Who then have we hurt more by our thoughtlessness and clumsiness than ourselves? Nondivers do not know what they are missing; it is we ourselves, the divers who have known the exquisite water world, who suffer from our own greed and carelessness.

To the Hunters. This book describes more than a dozen artificial reefs that have been established as fish havens (see listing in index). If you must hunt, please do so on one of these fishing reefs and take only what you need, leaving the larger fish to help sustain the populations. Spare the natural reefs so that they may enchant and captivate us on our next visit.

To the Photographers. Often one end of a photographer is "taking only pictures and leaving only bubbles," while the other end is doing serious fin damage to the reef. Please, use caution and show your appreciation of the magical, mystical marine environment with both ends of your body.

To All Divers. Let the octopus and the wolf eel stay on the reef where we can admire them and tell tales of them again and again. Let the big skate come and go as it pleases, surprising and thrilling us with each rare encounter. Join me in admiration of the curious ratfish and the efficient dogfish and let them remain in the sea.

The Sign of Peace. A new universal hand signal is emerging in our sport, which I hope will become as commonly seen as the "OK" sign. It is the Peace Sign, and its purpose is to encourage peace on the reef. Use it to remind buddies when they are careless with fin kicks. Use it to remind each other to not exceed fishing limits and to leave the large fish behind. Share the meaning of the peace sign with your dive club, dive buddies, and favorite dive shops. If you are a scuba instructor or dive master, include the teaching of this sign in your classes so that its meaning will become widely known.

Let us all remember that we are guests on the reef, that it is not ours to own or to abuse or to use for any reason other than to fill our minds with wonder.

Important Note. This book is not intended to be a training manual, instructional guide, or dive planning publication. Scuba diving is an activity with serious inherent dangers, and neither the author nor the publisher is implying, by listing sites in this book, that any of the sites are risk-free. Also, information in this book is based on facts available at press time and may be subject to change. Divers are responsible for their own safety, for developing their own dive plans and executing them based on prevailing conditions at the time and place of their impending dive as well as on their levels of experience and training. Neither the author nor the publisher accept responsibility for the safety of users of this book.

About This Book

Few areas of the underwater world can match the stunning beauty and dense sea life populations of Northwest waters. The cool waters and strong currents of Puget Sound and Hood Canal are home to an abundance of sea creatures, from vibrantly colored anemones to shadowy-gray wolf eels, tiny whelks to giant octopuses.

Northwest Boat Dives provides certified divers with an authoritative guide to dozens of exciting reefs and wrecks throughout Puget Sound and Hood Canal. Most of the dives are accessible only by boat and have never before been described in print. As scuba diving in general and Northwest diving in particular have grown over the past few years, many of the popular shore dive locations have become overcrowded. And although many divers have access to boat diving, most do not know where to find the environments they seek that are within their ability range. My purpose in researching, exploring, and compiling the information on the sites in this book was to provide divers with new and exciting dive site choices while offering insight into the ability and experience levels required, the hazards to be considered, and the sub-sea environment likely to be encountered. Whether you prefer drift diving, deep diving, night diving, wreck diving, or just touring an action-packed rock pile, you'll find sites in this book that fit your style and ability.

Boat Diving. Boat diving offers several advantages over shore diving. It gives divers unlimited access to far more reefs, easier entry and exit to the site, and it eliminates long surface swims. Also, by using a live boat pick-up system, divers can drift with the currents during tidal exchanges, covering far more area without the aggravation of long walks back to the starting point.

Little information has been published regarding boat dive sites and for obvious reasons. It is difficult, after all, to locate reefs and wrecks in open waters when directions to them must be given with landmarks. The arrival of Global Positioning Systems on the general market with very reasonable prices, some now under $150, has allowed mariners to pinpoint their location with fairly accurate latitude and longitude coordinates. The accuracy of G.P.S. receivers is controlled by the United States Department of Defense, which deliberately introduces a degree of error into the satellite signals called "selective availability." A "stand alone" G.P.S., for example, is expected to be accurate within 100 meters 95 percent of the time. How accurate it is within that 100 meters can fluctuate from exact, to 10 meters, to 50 meters, and so on.

A G.P.S. coupled with a Differential Beacon Receiver (D.B.R.), which was the configuration used to compile the coordinates in this book, is expected to be accurate within 5 to 10 meters 60 percent of the time. I have seldom had problems locating a reef using either of these systems. The addition of a "bottomfinder" or "fishfinder" to either system makes reef location a breeze. In order to make this book of value to all boat divers, I have included landmark and depth information to help those lacking electronics.

Just Add Water! The sixty dives described in this book can be visited by scuba divers who have achieved certification from one of the nationally or internationally recognized certifying agencies (see "Difficulty Ratings," below). Sites were selected based on the quantity of sea life present, underwater structure, and degree of difficulty. Each dive site is presented as follows:

"INFORMATION-IN-BRIEF": A boxed section at the beginning that provides the key data about the dive, including type of dive, general location, G.P.S. coordinates for the site and nearby towns or marinas, degree of difficulty (explained below in "Difficulty Ratings"), and "Tricky Stuff" (the most challenging aspects of the dive).

OVERVIEW: A preview of the highlights of each site and the type of reef (e.g., natural, artificial, wall, wreck).

THE DIVE IN DEPTH: Information to help divers determine if the site is within their ability and experience level; includes depth, current, and anchorage data as well as any suggested techniques for conducting the dive.

LOCATION: How to find the reef, where to launch, and location of airfills and gas docks. Also includes information regarding the geographical location of the dive site, including landmarks, buoys, and names of nearby coves, bays, islands, and other points of reference to assist divers in finding the site.

SUB-SEA ENVIRONMENT: A description, in nontechnical terms, of the site and the marine life likely to be encountered on the reef. This section does not attempt to encompass all of the life on the reef nor does it pretend to reflect an in-depth knowledge of marine biology. The verbal picture painted is designed merely to inform divers as to the types of sea life inhabiting the reef.

SEA LIFE: A recap of creatures living on the reef, in list format, to assist divers and photographers in choosing a site.

Difficulty Ratings. In the boxed section at the beginning of each dive is a category called "Degree of Difficulty," followed by one of three ratings: "All Divers" (includes beginning boat divers), "Intermediate," or "Advanced." To say all scuba divers fall into one of these three categories is oversimplification, for where are the dividing lines to be drawn?

Therefore, the difficulty ratings in this book are relative to *Northwest boat diving only.* If you have never made a boat dive or only a few, you are a beginning boat diver. If you have made several boat dives in the Northwest in various conditions, perhaps you are an intermediate. To visit the sites in this book rated as advanced, you should be skilled in dive planning and underwater navigation, and you should have experienced numerous Northwest boat dives in all kinds of conditions, including kelp beds, drift dives, deep dives, high boat traffic areas, and currents.

With the exception of drift dives, the difficulty ratings given in this book apply to dives conducted during slack current on calm waters. Due to changing conditions, divers must be responsible for evaluating conditions prior to entering the water and making final determinations on whether they have the experience and skill required to dive in the prevailing conditions.

The difficulty ratings for each dive are based on the following criteria:

ALL DIVERS = Divers who:
a. Are comfortable with boat diving in cold water.
b. Have developed good buoyancy control.
c. Are proficient at deep water exits and entries.
d. Can calculate slack current with proper adjustments.
e. Are in good physical condition.

INTERMEDIATES = Divers who:
a. Meet all of the above criteria.
b. Have made numerous boat dives.
c. Are experienced with deep diving (70–130 feet).
d. Can navigate underwater effectively.
e. Have had at least some experience swimming in currents.
f. Are comfortable with exiting and entering a "live boat."

ADVANCED = Divers who:
a. Meet all of the above criteria.
b. Are adept at all stages of dive planning,
   especially at "on-site" evaluation and plan adjustments.
c. Are experienced at drift diving and low-visibility diving.
d. Have completed a course in rescue diving.

Boat Diving Safety Procedures. When you begin boat diving, it is a good idea to visit the low-current sites and to have a boat operator on board while conducting your dive. Establish a well-planned procedure and require all divers to follow it when they dive from your boat or when you are supervising the activities. The best time to review procedures is during a pre-dive orientation prior to every dive. Your procedure should include a fifty foot, floating safety line attached to the stern of the boat, a well-displayed dive flag, routine anchor inspection on descent, and a method of retrieving or temporarily stowing weight belts and tanks at the end of each dive prior to reboarding. Everyone onboard should be shown how to start and operate the boat, and the boat should be equipped with a VHS radio or cell phone.

All diving, whether from boat or shore, should always be conducted in buddy teams.

Clarification of Terms.

LIVE BOAT: An unanchored, tended boat with the motor running, used to follow or drift with a dive team and pick up the divers at the end of their dive. Some of the sites in this book require a live boat scenario or they should not be attempted. On others, I have recommended a tended boat. This means an anchored boat with an operator on board who can pull or jetty the anchor, start the boat, and retrieve divers if they are unable to swim back to the boat. Some sites, especially some of those in Hood Canal, are easily dived from an anchored, untended boat. Still, boats with four divers (two buddy teams) always work out best.

FISH HAVEN: Many of the Washington State fishing reefs are designated on the NOAA navigational charts as fish havens. The terminology is used in this book to coincide with the charts only and not as a designator for marine sanctuaries or underwater parks.

FSW: Feet of salt water. Since divers are likely to dive at both slack before flood (low tide) and slack before ebb (high tide),the depth of sites in this book are given in ranges. Depending on what portion of the tide cycle divers plan their activities, they can expect the depth of the site to be somewhere in this approximate range.

Continuing Education. Regardless of which certifying agency you are affiliated with, the benefits of continuing education cannot be overstated. Every class, regardless of title, contributes additional skills to what I believe is the single most important ability of all, the ability to effect self-rescue. The knowledge, experience, and confidence gained from each dive completed and class attended help us to develop the ability to be more self-reliant in stressful situations. This ability is a huge asset to both us and our dive buddies. The truly great diver, however, is the diver who has all the mental and physical tools, as well as the training, to effect self-rescue, but who never has to use them, choosing instead to use good dive planning, physical conditioning, conservative dive practices, good buddy checks, well-maintained equipment, and common sense prior to diving.

Section One

North Puget Sound

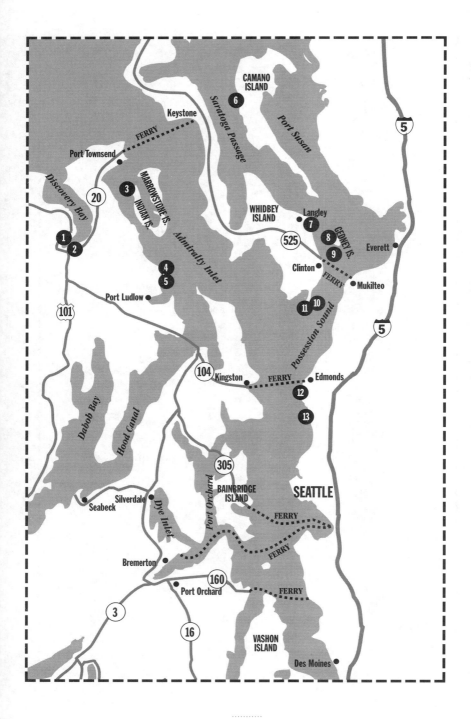

Ed's Fault (Woodmark Rocks)
• NORTH PUGET SOUND •

Dive Type: Natural rock reef
Location: Discovery Bay, Port Townsend area
Coordinates:
  Dive Site: 48-00-85 N
  122-50-36 W
  Port Townsend Marina: 48-06-40 N
  122-46-24 W
  Sequim Bay: 48-05-10 N
  123-01-60 W
Degree of Difficulty: All divers
Tricky Stuff: Finding the reef

Overview: Whatever type of geological activity may have created Ed's Fault (also known as Woodmark Rocks), an engrossing reef has developed on the rocky substrate, and a variety of marine plants and animals are comfortably at home here. Discovery Bay is a beautiful setting with vibrant blue-green waters surrounded by steep forested mountains. At the mouth of the bay lies Protection Island, which is now a bird sanctuary. Although it is illegal to venture onto the island, many of its puffins, terns, gulls, and herons visit Discovery Bay. You're also likely to see deer and bald eagles around the bay.

The Dive in Depth: All levels of boat divers should be comfortable at this site. Tidal exchanges create very little current in Discovery Bay, and the reef offers good visuals at all depths. Fishing boats do visit the reef, so display a dive flag and be on the lookout for discarded fishing line.

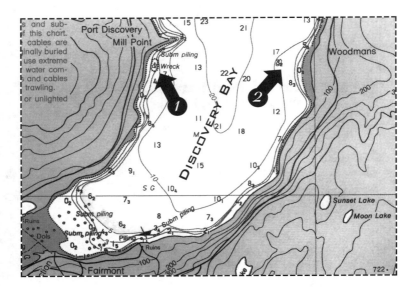

Location: This reef, located near the south end of Discovery Bay, can be difficult to locate without electronics. Boaters should easily find the reef using a G.P.S. or LORAN system. Boats equipped with a fishfinder or a depth sounder should also be able to locate the site, although it will probably take a little longer. The rocky rib runs north–south and is approximately 150 feet long. As you approach the southern shore of the bay, look for condominiums on the western shore and a house on the southern shore. To locate the reef, navigate west and southwest from the house at a compass heading of 240° to a depth of about 48 feet. Entering the water there should place you to the east of the reef; swim west, and the ridge should become evident. Gas, moorage, and boat launches are available in Sequim and Port Townsend. Air fills can be obtained in Port Townsend.

Sub-Sea Environment: The rock ridge rises from 90 fsw to 20 fsw, where it is shrouded with broadleaf kelp and kelp-dwelling creatures. Kelp greenlings, quillback rockfish, China rockfish, and black sea bass linger near the encrusted rocks, seeking their favorite snacks. Sea stars, sea urchins, strawberry and plumose anemones, and rock scallops paint the reef and make an intriguing backdrop for swarming schools of

Look for this house *southeast of Ed's Fault. Navigate from the house on a heading of 240° to locate the reef.*

perch. Huge boulders provide dens for giant octopuses, which live on the reef and feed on resident shellfish. Many members of the crab family scurry around on the rocks where leafy hornmouth snails, moon snails, and whelks graze. Look especially for hydroids on the flat sandy areas at the base of the reef. Blennies, eels, sculpins, and small ling cod also are found at this site.

Sea Life:

Anemones
Black sea bass
Blennies
Broadleaf kelp
China rockfish
Crabs
Decorator crabs
Eels
Flounders
Giant octopuses
Hermit crabs
Hydroids
Kelp crabs
Kelp greenlings

Leafy hornmouth snails
Ling cod
Moon snails
Plumose anemones
Quillback rockfish
Red rock crabs
Rock scallops
Sculpins
Sea stars
Sea urchins
Shiner perch
Strawberry anemones
Striped perch
Whelks

Shipwreck *Warhawk*
· N O R T H   P U G E T   S O U N D ·

Dive Type: Shipwreck
Location: Discovery Bay, Port Townsend area
Coordinates:
   Dive Site: 48-00-87 N
   122-51-47 W
   Port Townsend: 48-06-40 N
   122-46-24 W
   Sequim Bay: 48-05-10 N
   123-01-60 W
Degree of Difficulty: All divers
Tricky Stuff: None

Overview: This old sailing ship, reported to be about 180 feet in length, hauled freight throughout the late 1800s until she burned and sank in Discovery Bay in 1883. The *Warhawk* makes the perfect shallower second dive for those who have explored Ed's Fault (Woodmark Rocks, Dive #1) on their first dive of the day. The fault line dive and the *Warhawk* shipwreck dive are vastly different, and planning a two-tank day in Discovery Bay to visit these sites should be high on the to-do list of any Northwest diver. Bring a lunch and enjoy the scenic beauty both above and below the sparkling waters of this charming bay.

The Dive in Depth: This is a fine dive for all levels of scuba divers. The reef is shallow and currents are inconsequential. However, be sure to inspect the set of the anchor when starting your dive because winds can become substantial very quickly in Discovery Bay and a pulled-out anchor could result in a beached boat. Divers need to watch for sharp

Old Mill Point. *The* Warhawk *lies about 100 yards to the south.*

points among the rotting timbers and be aware of gauges and other dangling equipment that could become entangled in the debris as they swim over and around the wreck. Fishing boats do frequent the reef, so discarded fishing line, lost lures, and overhead boat traffic are other potential hazards.

Location: The *Warhawk* is located about 100 yards south of Old Mill Point in Discovery Bay (see chart on page 4). Two small signs on the shore advise boaters that the beaches are private property; the wreck is out from the southernmost sign. Using a depth sounder or fishfinder, start from Old Mill Point and locate a depth of 35 feet. Head southerly, paralleling the shoreline, and the wreck should show clearly on the depth sounder. No facilities of any kind are present in the immediate area, but fuel docks, moorage, restrooms, and boat launches are available at Sequim Bay and Port Townsend. Port Townsend also has a dive shop for air fills near the water at the marina south of the ferry dock.

Sub-Sea Environment: The disintegrating old hull lies on sand and wood particle substrate at a depth range of 28–38 fsw. The upper portions of the wreck, receiving good penetrating sunlight, are completely covered with white plumose anemones, which further reflect the light to brighten the entire area. A slow swim around and over the hull reveals the death of an artifact concurrent with the birth of a habitat. The *Warhawk* rests on her port side on a northeast-southwest line, somewhat perpendicular to shore. Colorful sun stars, sunflower stars, and mottled stars crawl up and down the rotting timbers, adding luster to the gloomy, silt-covered backdrop. Red Irish lords and mosshead warbonnets lie among the anemone. Striped perch and pile perch cruise the perimeter of the wreckage, pecking at morsels, while shiner perch, smartly dressed in glimmering silver, prefer to circle above the reef. Ling cod, greenlings, and black sea bass visit the remains of the *Warhawk* in search of meals and shelter. Also look for feather duster worms, octopuses, and countless other marine creatures on this rich and picturesque reef.

Sea Life:

Anemones	Mottled stars
Black sea bass	Nudibranchs
Blennies	Octopuses
Broadleaf kelp	Painted greenlings
Buffalo sculpins	Pile perch
Chitons	Quillback rockfish
Copper rockfish	Red Irish lords
Decorator crabs	Shiner perch
Feather duster worms	Snails
Flounders	Striped perch
Kelp crabs	Sun stars
Kelp greenlings	Sunflower stars
Ling cod	White plumose anemones
Mosshead warbonnets	

Alaska Reefer
• N O R T H   P U G E T   S O U N D •

Dive Type: Shipwreck
Location: Point Walan, Indian Island, Port Townsend area
Coordinates:
 Dive Site: 48-04-17 N
 122-44-71 W
 Port of Port Townsend: 48-06-40 N
 122-46-24 W
Degree of Difficulty: All divers
Tricky Stuff: Potential entanglement of gear

Overview: This site is a mess. That's what makes it such an interesting dive. The *Alaska Reefer,* formerly the USS *Pinton,* was converted to a refrigerator ship after World War II and served the commercial fishing industry. After a devastating fire in 1961, the *Reefer* sank just south of Point Walan, at the northeast end of Indian Island near Port Townsend. A large wooden barge, possibly used during salvage efforts on the *Reefer,* has sunk right next to the steel-hulled refrigerator ship—which reportedly went down on top of the wooden tug *Enola,* which had also burned and sunk here in 1911. The whole mess is now a reef that lies from 0 to 60 feet in depth.

The Dive in Depth: Negligible currents coupled with shallow depths make this an excellent site for beginning boat divers, novice wreck divers, and all night-divers. Remember, never attempt to penetrate any shipwreck unless you are a certified "wreck diver." The enormous extent of the wreckage offers intermediate and advanced divers an engrossing opportunity to gape at, and attempt to interpret, the bewildering chaos that is truly abundant here. Use extreme caution around the barge to avoid getting poked or having dangling equipment snagged by the myriad rotting protuberances. *Note:* This site is located on U.S. Navy property and requires permission from the Navy for civilian, recreational use. Normally permission is readily granted, but on occasion naval activities require the closure of the site. Divers may secure permission to trespass by calling 360-385-0100.

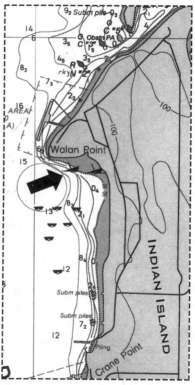

Location: The *Alaska Reefer* is located on the southern side of Point Walan at the northeast end of Indian Island. Approach the area slowly; the wreckage is shallow, and portions of it can usually be seen sticking out of the water. So much structure is present here that a depth sounder or fishfinder will easily identify the site. Anchor on the silty bottom, away from the wreckage; otherwise, your anchor line could become severely tangled and difficult to retrieve. Avoid an anchor-retrieval bounce dive by dropping anchor on the flat bottom on the east side of the whole mess, descend on the anchor line to check anchor position, and then swim to the barge, which lies east of the *Alaska Reefer*. Boat launches are available at Fort Flagler on Marrowstone Island, Mystery Bay State Park on Marrowstone Island, Fort Worden State Park at Port Townsend, and at the Port of Port Townsend, which also has a fuel dock. Air fills can be obtained in Port Townsend, close to the boat launch, and at Hadlock.

Sub-Sea Environment: The substructure of the *Alaska Reefer* lies on its port side, in a north-south line, at depths of 20 to 60 fsw. The starboard side of the 175-foot steel hull faces into the penetrating sunlight and is blanketed with white and orange plumose anemones. Several large, square openings on the main deck provide access for marine creatures to enter the hull. Take a dive light to inspect the encrusted innards through these openings. Sea stars are plentiful both within and without the *Reefer*'s hull as well as on the wooden barge. A mammoth winch is mounted atop the ruins of the sometimes-confusing wreckage, and cable is strewn about in tangles amid the wires and rusting bolts. Ling cod and kelp greenling swim around the debris while rockfish seek refuge in and around the holes and cracks. Perch school around the site and follow the divers who occasionally stir the aquatic stew enough to kick up easy meals for them. Red rock crabs and Dungeness crabs caretake the bottom, along with shrimp, moon snails, and nudibranchs. Always entertaining, schools of tube-snouts cruise by in their herky-jerky fashion, scouting the waters for plankton. The decaying barge lies on the east side of the *Alaska Reefer* and is visible at the surface except during very high tides.

Sea Life:

Blennies
China rockfish
Copper rockfish
Dungeness crabs
Flounders
Giant sea cucumbers
Kelp greenlings
Ling cod
Moon snails
Nudibranchs
Orange plumose anemones
Painted greenlings

Pile perch
Quillback rockfish
Red rock crabs
Sea stars
Shiner perch
Shrimp
Strawberry anemones
Striped perch
Tube worms
Tube-snouts
White plumose anemones

Klas Rock
• NORTH PUGET SOUND •

Dive Type: Natural rock reef
Location: East of Mats Mats Bay, Port Ludlow area
Coordinates:
   Dive Site: 47-57-70 N
   122-40-33 W
   Port Ludlow: 47-55-35 N
   122-40-80 W
   Port Townsend: 48-06-40 N
   122-46-24 W
Degree of Difficulty: All divers
Tricky Stuff: Approach, anchorage

Overview: This natural rock reef north of Port Ludlow is similar to The Sisters site (Dive #48) in Hood Canal, with resplendent beauty and brilliant colors providing the backdrop for the equally dazzling sea life on the reef. Klas Rock, Colvos Rock to the south, and other numerous shoals around these two large rocks are all interesting dive sites. Mats Mats Quarry (Dive #5) is also nearby. Plan an entire day for your visit here, if possible, and enjoy a two- or three-dive experience, all on natural reefs.

The Dive in Depth: Currents can be strong at Klas Rock during tidal exchanges, but a dive properly planned during slack current is suitable for all levels of divers. The bottom here is solid rock, so give the anchor time to set before entering the water and slide down the anchor line to ensure a firm hold before beginning your dive. The reef runs from 10 to 90 fsw, but most of its real beauty is in the shallower waters, above 50 feet. Making an ascent up the rock allows you to make a safety cruise at

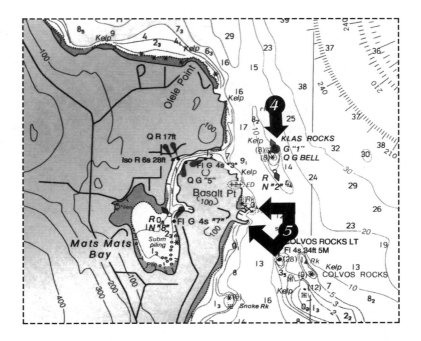

15 feet while enjoying the brilliant hues of the plants and animals that dwell in the kelp beds. As always, use caution when swimming in kelp areas and be aware of loose or dangling gear that might become entangled. Boat traffic is common around Klas Rock because of nearby Mats Mats Bay and the rock quarry to the west. An even greater hazard to boat divers approaching this site are the many rocks that are partially or fully submerged during high tide.

Location: Klas Rock is located near the mouth of Mats Mats Bay north of Port Ludlow (look for "Klas Rocks" on charts). It is often confused with the larger Colvos Rock; Klas Rock is near the northernmost navigational marker near Basalt Point, while Colvos Rock sports the southern navigational marker. Port Ludlow Marina has a gas dock, short- or long-term moorage, and a boat launch. Mats Mats Bay and Jefferson County Park to the north also have boat launches. The closest air fills are at Port Townsend.

Sub-Sea Environment: As divers descend past the upper, kelp-covered portions of the rock, the penetrating sunlight highlights the stunning beauty of the reef, revealing sponges, black pine coral, and bead corals. Nudibranchs and chitons slither across the seaweeds: porphyra, sea staghorn, bull kelp, and broadleaf kelp all grow on the reef. Cockscombs, warbonnets, and blennies seem to peer out from every small hole in the rocks, while rockfish and greenlings are abundant. Octopuses and small wolf eels inhabit the larger dens, so remember to bring your dive light. Anemones, flatfishes, red sea urchins, and communities of sea pens all share space at this aquarium-like site. Watch for curious seals, and at the surface check out the many sea birds that visit the rocks.

Sea Life:

Anemones	Ling cod
Barnacles	Nudibranchs
Bead coral	Octopuses
Black pine coral	Painted greenlings
Black rockfish	Porphyra
Blackeye gobies	Puget Sound rockfish
Blennies	Quillbacks
Broadleaf kelp	Red sea urchins
Bull kelp	Rock scallops
Cabezons	Sculpins
Chitons	Sea pens
Cockscombs	Sea staghorn
Copper rockfish	Sea stars
Crabs	Sponges
Flatfish	Warbonnets
Kelp greenlings	Wolf eels

Mats Mats Quarry
• NORTH PUGET SOUND •

Dive Type: Artificial reef boulders
Location: East of Mats Mats Bay, Port Ludlow area
Coordinates:
   Dive Site: 47-57-40
   122-40-50
   Port Ludlow: 47-55-30 N
   122-40-80 W
   Mats Mats Bay: 47-57-80 N
   122-40-20 W
   Port Townsend Marina: 48-06-40 N
   122-46-24 W
Degree of Difficulty: All divers
Tricky Stuff: Depth, approach

Overview: This is a working rock quarry, with tugs bringing barges in for loading and unloading. Immense cone-shaped rock piles serve as the north and south boundaries of the loading area for the quarry, and both piles are good dive sites. Their size, like the size of an iceberg, can be deceiving, with only the smaller portion of them being visible from the surface. The rock piles slope down to about 90 fsw, spreading widely in all directions.

The Dive in Depth: All levels of divers will enjoy this dive. Because the rock piles drop off fast, anchor close to one of them and swim to shore to start your dive. Descend to your desired depth and then explore the reefs from there back to the surface. Leave someone on board to guard against the wind or current swinging the boat into the rocks as it pivots on the anchor line. There is a large coil of cable on the north reef in about 30 feet of water, but it is lying flat and does not appear to be an entanglement threat. It is easy to become absorbed at this interesting dive site, so watch your depth and enjoy a 15-foot safety swim on your ascent. Tugs and barges use this quarry, so exercise caution and fly a dive flag. On one of our dives here a barge was in the process of loading; we told the tug captain of our intent and he gave us a two-hour window to complete our diving. Check the horizon and verify that there are no incoming barges before you begin your dive. Use caution entering and leaving the area by boat, since submerged rocks are shallow and numerous; navigate slowly and watch your depth sounder.

Location: This reef is easy to locate, north of Port Ludlow at Basalt Point on Mats Mats Bay (see chart on page 13). The quarry is on shore between Colvos Rock and Klas Rock. The dive sites are at the two ends of the U-shaped quarry, outside of the loading area. You will see many large rocks sticking out of the water, but beware of the many other large rocks that may be submerged, especially at high tide! Good anchorages are at the south side of the southern pile and at the north side of the northern pile. There are several boat ramps in the area, but most of them are usable only at high tide and have little parking. The Squamish Harbor boat launch is a 7-mile boat ride south of the site. Mats Mats Bay has a ramp that is adequate during high tide. The best launch sites are probably on Salisbury Point, just north of the east end of the Hood Canal Bridge, and at Port Townsend. The nearest air fills are in Port Townsend, Poulsbo, and Edmonds.

Sub-Sea Environment: Although this is in fact an artificial reef, the quarry has been in existence for a long time, and portions of the reef now have abundant marine life. In the shallows, broadleaf kelp shrouds the boulders. Clown nudibranchs, alabaster nudibranchs, gumboot chitons, and leafy hornmouth snails inhabit these upper parts of the reef, finding food and shelter in the kelp beds. Red rock crabs and hermit crabs scoot around on the rocks and ledges. Greenlings, sculpins, and perch are at home on the reef. Giant octopuses live in dens between the boulders, where they scatter broken crab shells on their porch steps.

Sponges, corals, and rock scallops add luster to the slate-colored reef. Water jellyfish, tube worms, limpets, and sea squirts are here, along with the myriad other marine animals and seaweeds you will surely find as you explore this interesting reef.

Sea Life:

Alabaster nudibranchs
Blood stars
Broadleaf kelp
Buffalo sculpins
Clown nudibranchs
Corals
Giant sea cucumbers
Giant octopuses
Gumboot chitons
Hermit crabs
Herring
Kelp greenlings
Leafy hornmouth snails
Limpets
Ling cod
Mottled stars

Orange plumose anemones
Painted greenlings
Pile perch
Quillback rockfish
Red Irish lords
Red rock crabs
Rock scallops
Sea squirts
Shiner perch
Sponges
Striped perch
Sun stars
Tube worms
Water jellyfish
White plumose anemones

Onamac Point
• North Puget Sound •

Dive Type: Artificial reef, boulders
Location: Camano Island, east of Whidbey Island
Coordinates:
Dive Site: 48-11-17 N
122-32-25 W
Langley Harbor: 48-02-44 N
122-24-25 W
Oak Harbor: 48-17-00 N
122-38-10 W
Degree of Difficulty: All divers
Tricky Stuff: Finding all the rock piles

Overview: Over the years, the state of Washington has created several artificial reefs in Puget Sound and Hood Canal to enhance bottom-fish habitat. This one is developing well, and each year the marine life on it becomes more populous. The reef consists of gigantic mounds of boulders in some places—some of them up to 20 feet high and over 40 feet long—and smaller mounds or even single boulders in other places. The reef is in beautiful Saratoga Passage, east of Whidbey Island, where waters are likely to be pleasant even on those days when wind waves are pounding into small-boat bottoms elsewhere around Puget Sound.

The Dive in Depth: Currents in this area are generally weak and variable. A slack-current dive from an anchored boat is possible, and all levels of divers will enjoy this site. The depth of the reef runs from 45 to 100 feet on a gently sloping bottom, allowing divers to choose their preferred depth limits. Small fishing boats frequent the reef, so beware of discarded fishing line in the area and watch for boat traffic during ascent. There is more than enough reef at this site for two dives; bring a lunch and two tanks of air.

Location: Onamac Point ("Camano" spelled backwards) is located in Saratoga Passage, on the west side and near the middle of Camano Island, east of Whidbey Island. The point itself is marked by a naviga-tional buoy, and currently a red-and-white can-type fishing buoy bobs in the water over the artificial reef. Air fills are available in Oak Harbor and Langley on nearby Whidbey Island, as are overnight moorage, gas, dockside services, and showers. Boat launches are at Coupeville, Oak Harbor, and Langley on Whidbey Island and at Camano Island State Park, Utsalady, and Maple Grove on Camano Island.

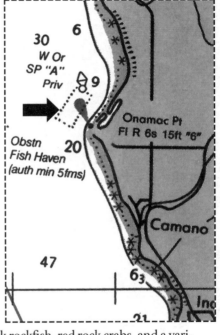

Sub-Sea Environment: Plu-mose anemones smother the rock tops and brighten the reef as they collect penetrating sunlight on their brilliant tentacles. Cracks and crevasses among the strewn boulders are plugged with quillback rockfish, red rock crabs, and a vari-ety of sea stars. Swimming around the rock piles, divers will encounter giant sea cucumbers prowling along the sandy bottom amid the flounders and Dungeness crabs. Skitterish kelp greenlings occasionally dart past, while the more complacent ling cod rest on the sandy bottom or atop the silty boulders in contemplation of visiting divers. Painted greenlings and schools of striped perch live on the reef, as do a vast spectrum of invertebrates. A slow ascent up the rock piles at the end of your dive will let you observe many colorful and industrious creatures carrying on their daily affairs, while giving you a chance to shed excess nitrogen. Many of the chinks and crannies among the rocks are deep and dark, so bring a dive light. Be sure to check the treetops on the bluff for bald eagles!

Sea Life:

Anemones
Blennies
Broadleaf kelp
Chitons
Dungeness crabs
Flounders
Giant sea cucumbers
Herring
Kelp greenlings
Ling cod

Moon snails
Nudibranchs
Painted greenlings
Plumose anemones
Quillback rockfish
Red rock crabs
Sea stars
Shiner perch
Striped perch

Langley Tire Reef
• N O R T H P U G E T S O U N D •

Dive Type: Artificial reef, tires
Location: Langley Harbor, east side of Whidbey Island
Coordinates:
  Dive Site: 47-02-44 N
  122-24-25 W
Degree of Difficulty: All divers
Tricky Stuff: None

Overview: Artificial reefs made from tires seem to develop slowly and to lack much of the marine life found on artificial reefs made of rock or concrete. But this is an exceptional tire reef. What is now the Langley Harbor Tire Reef began as the original breakwater for Langley Marina. Although that probably seemed like a good idea at the time, storms eventually converted the breakwater to what it is now: a well-developed

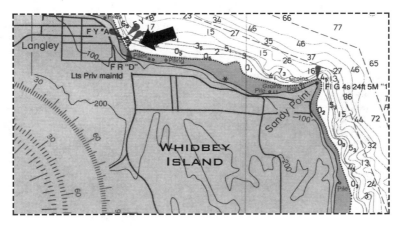

Langley Harbor entrance.

The tire reef lies adjacent to the breakwater pilings.

and heavily populated marine habitat. The reef is accessible by boat or from shore and, though it makes an excellent second dive following a deep first dive at either Possession Point (Dive #10) or the Possession Point Ferry wreck (Dive #11), divers selecting it as their primary site for the day won't be disappointed.

The Dive in Depth: This is an excellent dive for all levels of divers. Currents are very weak at this site, and the depth of the reef runs from 15 to 45 fsw. The north side of the reef extends west, under the fishing pier. Avoid this portion of the reef since fishers are likely to be on the pier casting and retrieving lures across the top of the reef there. Be cautious when swimming near the marina entrance and display a dive flag.

Location: The town of Langley is on the eastern side of Whidbey Island, and this reef is located outside of and adjacent to the existing Langley Marina breakwater. To approach the site from shore, go to the town of Langley, follow the signs to the marina, and walk along the northern side of the breakwater between the marina and the store. (Swimming out to the reef along this route would require you to pass beneath the fishing pier.) Begin your dive from the easternmost breakwater piling. The reef is somewhat semicircular from that point to the marina entrance. Boat divers have the luxury of simply tying up to the red-and-white mooring buoy outside the breakwater and beginning their dive from there. Air fills are available at the dive shop in the marina building, and it is permissible to moor to the gas dock for air fills. The Langley Marina also has a boat launch.

Sub-Sea Environment: Visibility is generally good on this reef, even in the summer months, if you dive at slack before ebb. The thousands of tires, many of them still strapped together, have collapsed to the seabed, where they are accompanied by a few old wooden piers. Large schools of striped perch and shiner perch seem to float just above the reef, dipping now and then to pick lunch off the encrusted tires. They're so plentiful that they'll often accompany you throughout your dive. Rockfish, red rock crabs, and shrimp peek out of the holes between the tires on the lookout for predators. Cabezons, ling cod, kelp greenlings, and black bass circle the reef, while the buffalo sculpins and red Irish lords remain content to witness the busy environment from their comfy vantage point. Many species of sea stars bring even more vibrancy to an already multicolored site. One side of the fallen breakwater rests next to the upright pilings that now form the present breakwater for the marina. A circular tour of the area brings you to the foot of these pilings where, in the shallows, kelp offers a variety of red, green, and brown hues to the penetrating natural light.

Sea Life:

Anemones	*Mottled stars*
Black bass	*Nudibranchs*
Blood stars	*Red Irish lords*
Broadleaf kelp	*Red rock crabs*
Buffalo sculpins	*Rockfish*
Cabezons	*Shiner perch*
Grunt sculpins	*Shrimp*
Gunnels	*Spider crabs*
Hydroids	*Striped perch*
Kelp greenlings	*Sun stars*
Leather stars	*Sunflower starfish*
Ling cod	*Wolf eels*

Gedney Barges
• NORTH PUGET SOUND •

Dive Type: Artificial reef, sunken barges
Location: Gedney Island (Hat Island), Everett area
Coordinates:
   Dive Site: 48-01-21 N
   122-19-28 W
   Langley Harbor: 48-02-44 N
   122-24-25 W
   Port of Everett: 47-58-90 N
   122-13-90 W
Degree of Difficulty: Intermediate
Tricky Stuff: Depth, boat traffic

Overview: Four barges, in various stages of decay, rest on the seabed just outside the entrance to this small marina and create an engrossing dive site. One barge is very much intact and appears to the novice to be still usable, with the exception of its negative buoyancy. The horizontal timbers of another have decayed, but the vertical timbers with small crossbeams remain, making this barge resemble a platform surrounded by grave markers. The site runs from 20 to 115 feet and is surrounded by a diversity of marine life. The substrate is a combination of sand and silt, peppered with decayed wood particles.

The Dive in Depth: Although this is an easy dive with little or no current, its inherent dangers make it unsuitable for novice divers. Depth is one consideration: the newest barge rests at depths from 70 to 115 feet at high tide, and the drop-off continues beyond recreational diving limits. Another serious hazard is that this reef is virtually under the

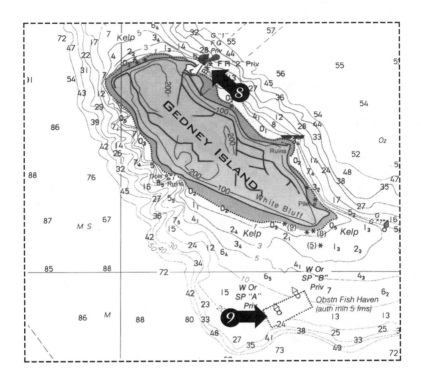

opening into the marina, and a buoyancy problem here could have serious consequences. Furthermore, an anchored boat flying a dive flag outside the marina entrance is too far from the actual site to alert entering boats of the presence of divers in the area. To make matters worse, a condemned barge floating at the surface bears a "KEEP OFF, NO DIVING" sign, which might imply to mariners that no diving of any type is conducted in the area.

Location: Gedney Island is located west of Everett and east of Whidbey Island. On the north side of this island is a small marina, with numerous houses on shore nearby. At the east side of this marina is a dilapidated old barge behind the breakwater. Anchor away from the barge toward the small crescent beach to the east of it. (The barge is private property, and moorage to it is prohibited.) Drop anchor in about

25 feet of water, descend the anchor line, and swim west toward the old floating barge. You will find the submerged barges to the north of the floating one. An excellent boat launch with several ramps, docks, and ample parking is on Marine View Drive in Everett. Gas, food, overnight moorage, showers, and air fills are available in Everett and Langley.

Sub-Sea Environment: Large schools of striped perch and pile perch swarm about the shallower portions of the reef and oversee the crab activities. The Dungeness crabs, who know how to party, have a hum-dinger in progress, and divers can get a quick lesson on "survival of the fittest" by simply observing about a hundred air-pounds worth of activity on the sandy bottom. Flounders spectate from the surrounding substrate, while painted greenlings hover nearby. Colorful sea stars are draped over all the barges, and an occasional ling cod can be seen moving in for lunch among the quillback rockfish. Although marine life is plentiful here, the most interesting part of this dive site is the structure of the reef itself. Divers can swim over, around, and partially under the wreckage. The most intact barge is also the deepest, and its two open hatchways give you a chance to peer into the hull with a dive light. Visible marine life is basically nonexistent inside, however, and an attempt to enter into this overhead environment is, therefore, groundless in addition to being dangerous.

Sea Life:

Dungeness crabs	*Quillback rockfish*
Ling cod	*Sea stars*
Mottled stars	*Striped perch*
Ochre stars	*Sun stars*
Painted greenlings	*Sunflower starfish*
Pile perch	

Gedney Reef
• North Puget Sound •

Dive Type: Artificial reef, concrete, and boulders
Location: Gedney Island (Hat Island), Everett area
Coordinates:
  Dive Site: 48-00-03 N
  122-18-62 W
  Port of Everett: 47-58-90 N
  122-13-90 W
  Langley Harbor: 48-02-44 N
  122-24-25 W
Degree of Difficulty: All divers
Tricky Stuff: Finding all the rock piles

Overview: Boulders of all sizes and shapes, long and narrow concrete slabs, and a variety of concrete hunks and chunks have been dumped south of this small island near Everett by the state of Washington to create fish habitat. Because the debris was dropped over a period of time, the reef reflects various stages of development in sustaining marine plant and animal life. The debris has been spread over an expansive area, so several repeat visits to various parts of the reef will provide divers an opportunity to inspect a vast variety of underwater landscapes and marine life.

The Dive in Depth: This is an excellent dive for all levels of divers. Although current is usually slight on the bottom during low tidal exchanges, surface current fluctuates from weak to robust during both flood and ebb, so if you dive at these times, leave someone on the boat to pick up divers if they should surface into challenging snorkel

Shellfish provide food *for many sea animals, including sea stars.*

conditions. All in all, slack current is the best time to dive this site. This is a fishing reef; watch for discarded fishing line and snagged lures on the rocks. Boat traffic can be heavy, so display a flag.

Location: The Gedney Reef is located 0.8 mile south of Gedney Island and 4 miles east of Everett (see chart on page 25). The nearest boat launches are at Everett and Marysville on the mainland and Langley Harbor on Whidbey Island. Air fills are available on the dock at Langley Harbor and in Everett. Both Everett and Langley have short-term and overnight moorage as well as gas docks, showers, and nearby restaurants.

Sub-Sea Environment: Scattered rock and concrete piles, from individual slabs to 20-foot-high pyramids, lie on a sandy bottom in 30–60 fsw. As you descend toward the sandy bottom, the glow from white plumose anemones catches your eye and draws you onto the reef. The typical visibility of 15–20 feet is good enough to allow these anemones to lure you from pile to pile with their ghostly glow. Several species of sea stars creep along the gloomy substrate, painting the gray backdrop with brilliant hues of purple, red, and yellow. Resident ling cod and cabezons cruise from roost to roost, and China rockfish and quillback rockfish stand guard at the openings of their hideouts. Perch and tube-snouts circle above the reef in scintillating schools. Giant octopuses, orange sea cucumbers, and California sea cucumbers inhabit the reef as the shy ratfish, flounders, and sand-loving big skates observe from the perimeter. Take a dive light to peer into the many dark holes between the rocks and tour the tops of the tall pyramids as you near the end of your dive for a scenic safety stop. Moving off the reef to throw some crab rings during your surface interval can be a rewarding diversion.

Sea Life:

- *Big skates*
- *Cabezons*
- *California sea cucumbers*
- *China rockfish*
- *Dungeness crabs*
- *Flounders*
- *Giant octopuses*
- *Ling cod*
- *Mottled stars*
- *Ochre stars*
- *Orange sea cucumbers*
- *Pile perch*
- *Quillback rockfish*
- *Ratfish*
- *Red rock crabs*
- *Shiner perch*
- *Striped perch*
- *Sun stars*
- *Sunflower sea stars*
- *Tube-snouts*
- *White plumose anemones*

Possession Point
• NORTH PUGET SOUND •

Dive Type: Wall dive
Location: South end of Whidbey Island
Coordinates:
Dive Site: 47-54-21 N
122-22-57 W
Langley Marina: 48-02-44 N
122-24-25 W
Everett Marina: 47-58-90 N
122-13-90 W
Degree of Difficulty: Intermediate
Tricky Stuff: Currents, depth

Overview: The natural rock structure of this site is simply phenomenal. Silty sediment covers a series of rock walls and valleys that provide habitat for myriad saltwater creatures. Huge chasms and crevasses wind mazelike around the walls, creating a rugged and scenic seascape for divers to explore. Layers of shelves carved into sandstone and rock, and ledges filled with mysterious holes and cracks, inspire divers to peer into them with a dive light to discover whatever secrets might lie deep within. To travel to this site with only one tank of air brings about remorse and makes you determined to return. Although marine life here is not abundant, there is plenty to see, and the structure itself is quite overwhelming. While on the boat, keep an eye out for bald eagles in the trees along the shore.

The Dive in Depth: Depth and surface currents make this an intermediate to advanced dive site. Bottom current is less than surface current on this reef, but dives must still be planned for slack, since the surface current can quickly carry divers away from the steep walls near shore and leave them hovering over deep, dark nothingness a short distance away. The depth of the reef runs from 20 to over 100 feet, and the underwater terrain continues to drop off to over 200 feet quite quickly. A tended boat is recommended in case divers need to be picked up in surface currents. As always, fly a dive flag, since salmon-fishing boats frequent the east side of Whidbey Island after other salmon-fishing areas close.

Location: This site is located on the southeast corner of Possession Point on Whidbey Island (see chart on page 34). Find the southernmost house on the southeast corner of the island and look for a dirt bluff 150 yards or so south of the house. At low tide, a huge rock can be seen on shore, and the site is directly out from the rock. Using a depth sounder, approach the bluff and watch for the 200-foot bottom to jump up rapidly as you near shore. If using a G.P.S., punch in the coordinates, and have a pre-dive sandwich on your way to the reef. Anchor close in at a depth of 30 to 40 feet and descend the wall to your preferred depth. The bottom is rock, so inspect the anchor on descent. Moorage, gas, food, and air fills are nearby in Everett or at the Langley Marina. Boat launches nearby include Port of Everett, Port of Edmonds, and Kingston Marina. All three offer guest docks for day or overnight use, restrooms with showers, and nearby restaurants.

Sub-Sea Environment: Rappelling down the anchor line or making a free descent from a live boat into the shallows of the reef brings divers face to face with the tiny shrimp, nudibranchs, snails, and gunnels that inhabit the broadleaf kelp and coral-coated rocks. Schools of shiner perch and all sizes of striped perch whirl and dart above the seaweeds in sizable numbers. Plumose anemones cast their ghostly glow from atop gloomy, gray boulders and bedrock as you approach the upper rim of the walls where mottled sea stars, ochre sea stars, and sun stars are also often draped. Red rock and Dungeness crab are at home on the reef along with hermit crabs and spider crabs. Ling cod, kelp greenlings, and painted greenlings are in attendance throughout the site as are both white and orange sea cucumbers and giant sea cucumbers.

Touring along the nearly vertical walls, divers can peek into the zillions of cracks and crevasses with a dive light and perhaps confront one of the solitary octopuses or sea bass that repose in the depths seeking privacy until mealtime. The "fingers" of the reef meander along changing directions continuously while basically running from north to south above a very deep bottom. Large, yet insubstantial, caves exist along the deep walls and beckon underwater lookey-loos to poke a curious nose inside. Follow a well-prepared dive plan when visiting this site, and enjoy a 3-minute safety stop in the variegated shallows at the end of your dive.

Sea Life:

Broadleaf kelp	*Orange sea cucumbers*
Corals	*Painted greenlings*
Dungeness crabs	*Plumose anemones*
Giant sea cucumbers	*Red rock crabs*
Gunnels	*Sea bass*
Hermit crabs	*Shiner perch*
Kelp greenlings	*Shrimp*
Ling cod	*Snails*
Mottled sea stars	*Spider crabs*
Nudibranchs	*Striped perch*
Ochre sea stars	*Sun stars*
Octopuses	*White sea cucumbers*

Possession Point Ferry
• NORTH PUGET SOUND •

Dive Type: Sunken ferryboat
Location: South end of Whidbey Island
Coordinates:
   Dive Site: 47-53-82 N
   122-23-59 W
   Port of Everett: 47-58-90 N
   122-13-90 W
   Port of Edmonds: 47-48-62 N
   122-23-53 W
   Langley Harbor: 48-02-44 N
   122-24-25 W
Degree of Difficulty: Intermediate
Tricky Stuff: Currents, depth

Overview: This old ferry, the *Kehloken*, lies on a north-south line near the southern end of Possession Point, Whidbey Island, at depths of 60 to 80 feet. The ship began her public service as a passenger ferry in California, matured into a popular Northwest waterfront restaurant, and after a damaging fire, was retired to the bottom of Puget Sound in 1983. Unable to change her helpful ways, the *Kehloken* has spent her retirement serving the public as a fishing reef with plenty of snags and a popular scuba-diving site. The rudder is still intact, and a huge turbine is visible as you swim over the top of the ruins. The ferry is impossible to explore in its entirety on a single swim-through, so plan a two-tank visit to this site. Underwater photographers will be well rewarded if they catch this dive site on a good-visibility day, while surface photographers may get a chance to capture one of the resident bald eagles on film.

The Dive in Depth: Because of its depth, this site should be considered an intermediate to advanced dive. Watch below as you approach the wreckage: many sharp and rusty parts of the ferry structure stick up on top of the wreck waiting to poke or snag a descending diver. A well-planned dive profile and a 15-foot safety stop are mandatory here. Allow an adequate surface interval if you are planning a two-tank visit to the site. This is a Washington State artificial fishing reef, so you're likely to encounter tangles of discarded fishing line. Furthermore, the Possession Point Ferry is one of the more popular boat dives in Puget Sound, so display a flag and surface cautiously. Dive at slack current, and leave a deckhand on the boat to round you up in case you surface into challenging snorkel conditions.

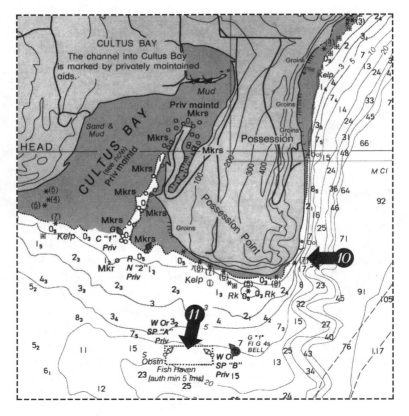

Location: This artificial reef is located south of Possession Point, Whidbey Island. From the green bell buoy travel 0.3 mile at 260° and watch your depth sounder. The ferry is substantial and will show clearly on good fishfinders that show bottom contour. Boat launches nearby include Port of Everett, Port of Edmonds, and Kingston Marina. All three offer guest docks for day or overnight use, restrooms with showers, and nearby restaurants. The nearest air fills are in Everett, in Edmonds, and at the Langley Marina on Whidbey Island.

Sub-Sea Environment: A beautiful community of orange and white plumose anemones thrives on the wreck. China rockfish and quillback rockfish play peek-a-boo from the nooks and crannies of the ferry, while resident ling cod observe divers from their resting places. Shy ratfish are plentiful here, and surrender to their snoopy ways by following divers at a distance and watching with those big round eyes as their curious visitors blow bubbles. Schools of striped perch and pile perch hang out just over your head. Sunflower sea stars, mottled stars, ochre stars, and sun stars lend their vibrant colors to the rusty old boat, along with orange cucumbers and giant sea cucumbers. Red rock crabs stow away in the hidey-holes around the deck, where hermit crabs and decorator crabs may also be found.

Sea Life:

China rockfish
Christmas anemones
Decorator crabs
Dungeness crabs
Flounders
Giant sea cucumbers
Hermit crabs
Ling cod
Moon snails
Mottled stars
Ochre stars

Orange cucumbers
Orange plumose anemones
Pile perch
Quillback rockfish
Ratfish
Red rock crabs
Striped perch
Sun stars
Sunflower sea stars
White plumose anemones

Edmonds Oil Dock
• NORTH PUGET SOUND •

Dive Type: Artificial reef, pilings
Location: Edmonds area
Coordinates:
Dive Site: 47-48-21 N
122-23-88 W
Edmonds Marina: 47-48-62 N
122-23-53 W
Degree of Difficulty: All divers
Tricky Stuff: Currents

Overview: Although it's also accessible from shore, diving the Edmonds oil dock from a boat either eliminates a long surface swim or extends dive time under the dock itself. The oil dock, no longer in use, is supported by dozens of pilings that are surrounded by and covered with an abundance of marine life. This is a marine preserve and, as such, is a superb site for beginning photographers to practice both wide-angle and macro techniques, with cooperative and lively animals in a splendid setting rich with vibrant colors. If you catch this dive on a good-visibility day, it's like diving in an aquarium.

The Dive in Depth: This is a good site for all levels of divers. Currents can get quite rapid during tidal exchanges, so dive this site only at slack current. The bottom drops off quickly to the west as you leave the protection of the pilings, and this western end of the dock is also an area of heavy boat traffic because of the nearby Edmonds small-boat marina. If you plan to explore outside the pilings, navigate carefully and return to the pilings or the east side of the dock to make your ascent.

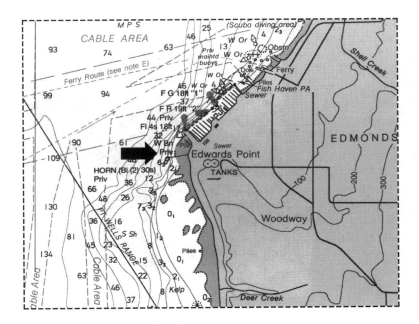

Location: The Edmonds oil dock is located at Edwards Point, just south of the Edmonds small-boat marina. A long row of pilings leads from the shore to the oil dock. The dive site is under the rectangular dock, which runs north to south, parallel to shore. To approach the site from land, either submerge near shore and enjoy the sea life around the pilings on the swim out to the dock or surface-swim along the pilings and descend at the fuel dock to begin your dive. When diving by boat, anchor on the southeast side of the fuel dock for protection from boat traffic, boat wakes, and wind, and descend on the anchor line or one of the pilings to begin your dive. This plan also provides a good point of reference for novice underwater navigators to easily return to their boat. The Edmonds Marina offers boat launching, dining, temporary and overnight moorage, and a fuel dock. Air fills are available in Edmonds and Lynnwood.

Sub-Sea Environment: White plumose anemones cloak the lower portions of the pilings, sharing their territory with sun stars, mottled stars, barnacles, and small sculpins. Striped perch and pile perch school around the pilings and follow the crab wars in progress on the bottom, picking off tiny morsels of spilled shellfish. Tangles of tube worms wave their feathery plumes as they take their food from the passing currents, and flounders nearly disappear from sight as they park on the matching sands. Painted greenlings, kelp greenlings, and small ling cod are all present on the reef. Moon snails, nudibranchs, sea pens, sponges, and sea cucumbers coexist on the sandy bottom. You may see several species of spider crabs, red rock crabs, Dungeness crabs, and hermit crabs. Old discarded pipes, valves, and other metal debris are littered about outside the pilings and are gradually becoming life-bearing portions of the reef. Depth beneath the pilings runs from 40 to 60 feet from the north end to the south end of the pier. To the north of the dock, the sandy bottom gives way to a rocky area at about 80 feet. South of the dock, at a depth of 60–70 feet, is a tire reef on which octopuses make dens.

Sea Life:

Barnacles
Buffalo sculpins
Cabezons
Crabs
Dungeness crabs
Flounders
Hermit crabs
Kelp greenlings
Ling cod
Moon snails
Mottled stars
Nudibranchs
Octopuses
Painted greenlings

Pile perch
Red Irish lords
Red rock crabs
Rockfish
Sea cucumbers
Sea pens
Spider crabs
Sponges
Striped perch
Sturgeon poachers
Sun stars
Tube worms
White plumose anemones

Reef at Boeing Creek
• NORTH PUGET SOUND •

Dive Type: Artificial reef, boulders and concrete
Location: South of Edmonds
Coordinates:
Dive Site: 47-45-09 N
122-23-16 W
Edmonds Marina: 47-48-62 N
122-23-53 W
Armeni Ramp, Elliott Bay: 47-35-38 N
122-22-54 W
Degree of Difficulty: All divers
Tricky Stuff: Surface currents

Overview: This site, also called "The Trees" by local fishermen, is another of the several artificial fishing reefs created by the state of Washington. Now well developed and boasting an extensive assortment of marine life, it's just a couple of miles south of Point Wells, making it quite convenient for both Seattle and North End divers. Boulders of various sizes and a few large concrete slabs have been dropped in sizable piles, parallel to shore, north to south, in 50 to 80 feet of water about 200 feet out from the beach.

The Dive in Depth: This is a good site for all levels of divers. Even though this reef is near the shore, where currents are generally weaker than in midchannel, plan your visit here during slack current unless you are using a live boat; the surface currents are stronger than the bottom currents and are often impossible to swim against during tidal exchanges. The north-south layout of the reef is fairly easy for the less-experienced

diver to navigate. The east side of
the site is shallow and the west
side deeper, so any diver can find
his or her comfort zone. This is a
fishing reef, so expect boat traffic
and discarded fishing line.

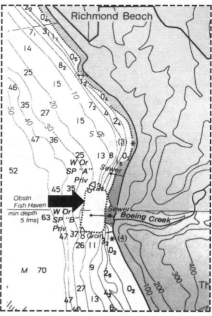

Location: As at all Washington fishing reefs, a red-and-white
can-type fishing buoy may or
may not be present. This artificial reef lies 2.1 miles south of
Point Wells and 4.5 miles south
of Edmonds. A pointed bluff on
shore, slightly south of the site,
is topped by two red trees and
a house with a prominent deck
structure. This bluff is one landmark divers can look for to help
locate the reef. Another landmark is a very small railroad bridge over
Boeing Creek, also just south of the site. An adequate fishfinder set at –2
or –3 sensitivity easily defines the region of rubble to be explored. Locate
the Boeing Creek confluence and, using the fishfinder, navigate slowly
north over a 50-foot bottom. The reef should become evident after a few
minutes of searching. A handheld G.P.S. unit set to the proper coordinates will place divers over the reef even more quickly. Day use and
overnight guest moorage and two boat slings for launching are available
at Edmonds Marina, with restaurants and showers nearby. Two boat
launches are south of the site, in Elliott Bay: the Shilshole ramp in the
north and the Armeni ramp in the south of the bay. Both Edmonds and
Elliott Bay have fuel docks. Air fills are available in Edmonds and Seattle.

Sub-Sea Environment: The debris appears to have all been dumped
on the sandy bottom at the same general time, as the area reflects a
consistent stage of development into a living reef. The underwater landscape is varied enough to provide habitats for many small sea creatures

The reef lies *out from the bluff on the left.*

and some sizable fish. Each hole and channel between the rocks and slabs is a fascinating environment to examine with a dive light and becomes a perfect little stage on which to photograph its myriad inhabitants. Small rocks scattered up the eastern, shallower side of the reef provide an interesting swim on ascent. Though a first swim-through may leave the impression that you have "been there, done that," take time to investigate the nooks and crannies for insight into the daily lives of their residents. A second visit to a different part of the site can also be rewarding. Decorator crabs seem to dwell in every hollow and cavity among the rocks. A neighborhood of red sea urchins is developing on the south end of the reef, and gumboot chitons are plentiful. Copper rockfish, quillback rockfish, ling cod, and kelp greenlings are residents here. A short swim to the surrounding sandy bottom reveals good-sized Dungeness crabs sharing the territory with English sole. Giant sea cucumbers, orange sea cucumbers, shrimp, tube worms, and tube-snouts are also commonly found at this dive site.

Sea Life:

Copper rockfish	*Kelp greenlings*	*Red rock crabs*
Crescent gunnels	*Ling cod*	*Shiner perch*
Decorator crabs	*Orange sea cucumbers*	*Shrimp*
Dungeness crabs	*Orange plumose*	*Tube worms*
English sole	*anemones*	*Tube-snouts*
Giant sea cucumbers	*Quillback rockfish*	*White plumose*
Gumboot chitons	*Red sea urchins*	*anemones*

Section Two

Central Puget Sound

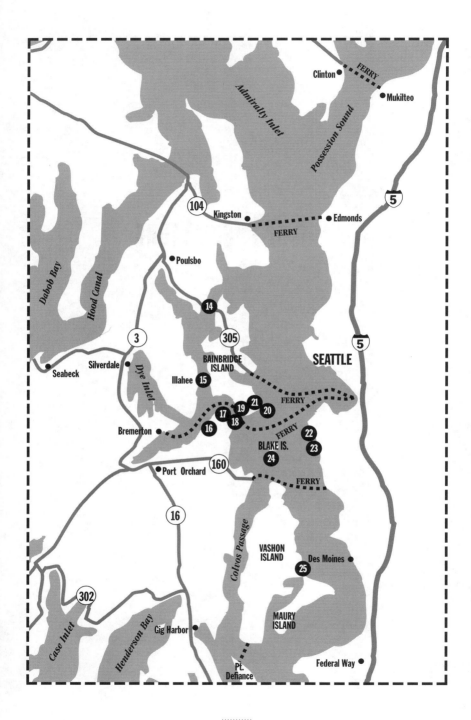

Agate Passage
• C E N T R A L   P U G E T   S O U N D •

Dive Type: Drift Dive
Location: Northwest end of Bainbridge Island
Coordinates:
  Dive Site: 47-42-78 N
  122-23-88 W
  Poulsbo: 47-43-88 N
  122-38-95 W
Degree of Difficulty: Intermediate
Tricky Stuff: Buddy contact

Overview: Two buddy teams, a live boat, and a substantial tidal exchange are the only ingredients needed to have too much fun on this exhilarating dive at the northwest end of Bainbridge Island. Diving buoy-to-buoy takes about a half hour. By slightly reducing the distance, you can make two or even three drifts through the passage on one tank of air (depending on air consumption). A handheld 3-foot piece of rope with a knot in each end removes the aggravation of buddy separation and even allows a little "crack the whip" action that adds even more fun to a dive that already has you giggling through your regulator. Visibility is usually pretty good along the bottom; there is much to see, and only an occasional fin kick is necessary to perfect your course or adjust your position with your buddy. Because this is a shallow area, the Agate Passage dive makes an excellent second dive after a visit to one of the deeper dive sites around Bainbridge Island. This dive site is also accessible from shore.

The Dive in Depth: This is a great first drift dive for intermediate divers. The bottom is flat and predictable, with a maximum depth of less than 45 feet. The wider waters of Port Orchard to the south and Port Madison to the north cause the currents to slow substantially for a less-challenging, deep-water exit back onto the live boat. Boat traffic through Agate Passage, which is very heavy at times, presents the biggest hazard to drifting divers. Clearly display a dive flag on the boat, and have the boat operator position the boat near the divers and between the divers and oncoming boat traffic when possible. Buddy teams should stay on bottom until ready to surface, remembering to listen, look up, and reach up when nearing the surface on ascent. As mentioned above, a short, 3-foot section of rope with a knot in each end for divers to hold helps reduce the possibility of buddy separation, which would require divers to surface mid-channel. The rope should be hand held and not tied or attached to divers or their equipment.

Location: Agate Passage lies between Port Madison and Port Orchard, beneath the bridge at the northwest end of Bainbridge Island. Channel-marker buoys are evident both north and south of the bridge and present reasonable drift boundaries. Boat-launch sites are plentiful around Bainbridge Island, including ramps at Poulsbo, Keyport Marina, Suquamish, Fay-Bainbridge State Park, and Miller Bay. To reach the bridge from land, follow Hwy 305 north from Winslow or south from Poulsbo. The nearest

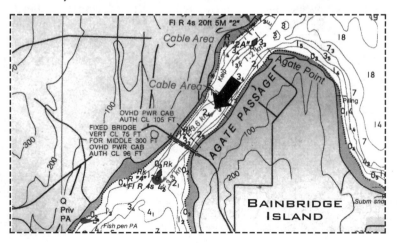

air fills are in Poulsbo; divers can also obtain air fills in Bremerton, Winslow, and Seattle.

Sub-Sea Environment: The high currents keep the rocky bottom swept clean, and small creatures abound among the cobblestones and on the larger rocks near the bridge. Carpets of tiny white sea anemones cloak the boulders and brighten the bottom as you fly past them. Myriad starfish are draped about on the rocky and shell-strewn passage floor, and red rock crab hunch down to take what little shelter is available from the

A tangle *of tubeworms.*

sweeping currents. Several sculpin species also manage to thrive in the rapid currents amid the tube worms and barnacles. As you drift over the cobblestone bottom, you'll encounter occasional anemone-covered boulders protruding into your fly zone. Taking an extra-deep breath to fill your lungs to capacity will provide the additional buoyancy required to rise above the boulders long enough to pass over them. It takes a little practice to get the timing just right, but if you haven't mastered the technique after the first drift through the passage...hey...do it again! Just don't hold your breath.

This is also a very scenic dive during slack current. Not quite as much fun, perhaps, but the frilly anemones number in the billions, and colorful corals and sponges are prevalent.

Sea Life:

Corals	*Sponges*
Red rock crabs	*Starfish*
Sculpins	*Tube worms*
Sea anemones	

Illahee Town Dock
• CENTRAL PUGET SOUND •

Dive Type: Artificial reef, tires
Location: Port Orchard Passage, north of Bremerton
Coordinates:
  Dive Site: 47-36-47 N
  122-35-41 W
  Bremerton: 47-34-20 N
  122-37-20 W
  Poulsbo: 47-43-90 N
  122-38-95 W
Degree of Difficulty: All divers
Tricky Stuff: None

Overview: Tires! Tires! Tires! Must be ten thousand of them composing this artificial reef. Rows of tires and piles of tires placed near the end of the town pier to enhance fishing have become home to a conglomeration of sea life. Although there are tire reefs of all sizes around Puget Sound, the town of Illahee is to be commended on having built one big, serious tire reef at the end of its dock. This shallow site is a short distance north of several deeper Rich Passage dive sites, so give it serious consideration as a second dive. Additionally, all of the Rich Passage sites are "slack-current only" sites, again making this reef a logical selection as a second site once the current has begun to run again. This site can be approached as a boat dive or from shore.

The Dive in Depth: Out of the main flow of current, not very deep, and diveable from the end of the dock as well as by boat, this is an excellent location for less-experienced or newly certified divers to practice

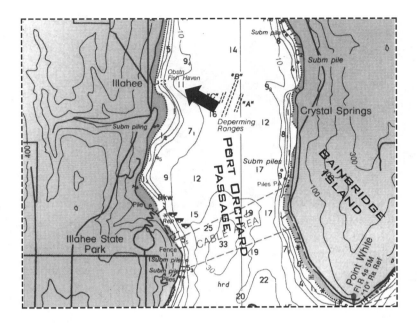

buoyancy control or to improve their other skills while having a pleasant dive and a good visual experience. There is small boat traffic in the area and this is a fishing reef, so display a dive flag and listen for motors during ascent. Fishing line is also likely to become part of the reef now and then, as anglers get their lures captured by pesky recaps.

Location: This reef is right off the end of the Illahee town dock, on the west side of Port Orchard Passage. Shore divers can approach on foot from town. Boat divers can tie up and dive from the dock or anchor out from the end of the dock and enter the water from the boat. Air fills and dockside services are available in Bremerton, to the south, and Poulsbo, to the north. The nearest boat launch is at Illahee State Park, less than a mile south. The Poulsbo Marina has short-term and overnight moorage and a gas dock. The shopping district, a short walk from the marina, has restaurants and marine supplies.

Sub-Sea Environment: The tires have been positioned in long rows

Illahee town dock. *The tire reef is east of the dock and easily reached by boat or from the dock as a shore dive.*

parallel to the shore as well as stacked in gigantic, random piles. Every tire has a few resident shrimp peering out at passing divers, and most have a red rock crab or two clinging to them. Orange and white plumose anemones adorn the black background with their bright and feathery tentacles. Red Irish lords and other sculpins inhabit the reef as do sea stars, chitons, and an occasional sea pen. Perch school above, and C-O sole rest on the sand. Sea lemons and alabaster nudibranchs are also tenants. Although this reef lacks the quantity of big fish and the bright colors found elsewhere in the Sound, the site is worth a visit from curious divers who want to see a really big tire reef and examine the creatures and plants that inhabit one.

Sea Life:

Alabaster nudibranchs	Red Irish lords
C-O sole	Sculpins
Decorator crabs	Sea lemons
Gumboot chitons	Sea pens
Lined chitons	Shrimp
Mottled stars	Striped perch
Orange plumose anemones	Sun stars
Pile perch	Sunflower sea stars
Red rock crabs	White plumose anemones

Waterman Lighthouse
• CENTRAL PUGET SOUND •

Dive Type: Natural rock reef
Location: West end of Rich Passage, east of Bremerton
Coordinates:
  Dive Site: 47-35-11 N
  122-34-24 W
  Manchester Boat Ramp: 47-33-21 N
  122-32-58 W
  Bremerton: 47-34-20 N
  122-37-20 W
  Port Orchard Marina: 47-32-70 N
  122-38-35 W
Degree of Difficulty: Advanced
Tricky Stuff: Currents, depth

Overview: Rapid currents and a massive bedrock substrate combine to make this site a choice location for Puget Sound marine life to seek food, shelter, and companionship. In addition to several fish species, the crustaceans and other invertebrates present on the reef offer excellent opportunities for both macro and wide-angle photography. The currents here are tricky, so don't forget to monitor your compass and gauges closely.

The Dive in Depth: Because of depth and tricky currents, this natural rock reef is an advanced dive. It should be attempted only during slack current before ebb because the waterfall current here can take a diver down to 140 feet or so before it lets go. It is also quite common for the surface current and the bottom current to be running in opposite

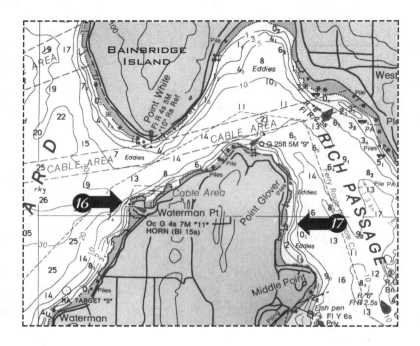

directions, and current strength increases at depth. Swimming into the current at 50 feet, for example, can be fairly easy, but drop down a couple more ledges to 65 feet or so, and swimming against the current becomes impossible. Each ledge seems to drop down to the west and down to the south at the same time, so even staying on the same ledge will inconspicuously keep taking a diver deeper. The ledges drop off very fast and exceed the safe limits for recreational divers, so constant monitoring of your depth gauge cannot be overemphasized. A live boat scenario is the best way to plan dives at Waterman Point. An alternative is to have someone on board to release the anchor line and make a live pick-up, if necessary. The tidelands here are all private property; please respect the rights and privacy of the local homeowners. Anchor out from the navigational marker in at least 20 feet of water to begin your dive.

Location: Not really a lighthouse, the Waterman navigational light is located on Waterman Point on the west side of Point Glover, north of

Sinclair Inlet and the entrance to Dyes Inlet. Anchor near the marker in about 40 feet of water and descend on the anchor line to check the set of the anchor, since the bottom is all rock here. Start your dive by swimming into whatever slight current may still be present at slack, and note any directional changes the current may make during your dive. Boat launches are at the town of Manchester on the east side of Point Glover, at Port Orchard, which also has a fuel dock, and at the Evergreen City Park boat ramp in Bremerton. Restaurants and air fills are available in Bremerton.

Sub-Sea Environment: Sea life abounds on this reef, as on most natural rock reefs in high-current areas of Puget Sound. Each solid rock ledge provides habitat, and fissures and gaps among the ledges create dens for all the creatures seeking protection from predators and sweeping currents. Giant barnacles blanket the rocks, assisted by mottled sea stars, sun stars, leather stars, and blood stars. Decorator crabs bravely raise their tiny pincers in defense when struck by the beam of an intruding dive light, then scurry into some dark hole seeking shelter. Thousands of shrimp flit in reverse among the scallops and orange cucumbers. Moon snails slip along among their scattered egg casings on a substrate of broken shells. Sculpins and greenlings are plentiful on the busy reef, along with larger fish including ling cod and cabezons.

Sea Life:

Blood stars	*Mottled sea stars*
Buffalo sculpins	*Northern ronquils*
Cabezons	*Northern sculpins*
Clams	*Orange cucumbers*
Decorator crabs	*Orange nudibranchs*
Giant barnacles	*Painted greenlings*
Grunt sculpins	*Quillback rockfish*
Gunnels	*Red rock crabs*
Hermit crabs	*Scallops*
Kelp greenlings	*Shrimp*
Leather stars	*Striped perch*
Ling cod	*Sun stars*
Moon snails	*White nudibranchs*

Wautauga Beach
• CENTRAL PUGET SOUND •

Dive Type: Natural rock reef
Location: Rich Passage, Point Glover, east of Bremerton
Coordinates:
   Dive Site: 47-35-13 N
   122-32-51 W
   Bremerton: 47-34-20 N
   122-37-20 W
Degree of Difficulty: Intermediate
Tricky Stuff: Currents, anchorage

Overview: Located in Rich Passage, where currents virtually rush during tidal exchanges, this reef offers the multitude of sea life common to high-current areas of Puget Sound. The bedrock on the shore shows you what kind of topography to expect underwater. The current keeps the rocks swept clean and feeds the abundant marine life found on the reef.

The Dive in Depth: Touring this site is possible only at slack current; at any other time this becomes a drift dive. A drift dive will allow only a brief view of the main portion of the reef, but the surrounding areas of sand and stones are so well inhabited that drifting the site considerably amplifies the experience. However, plan a drift dive here only on an ebb current from Point Glover toward Middle Point, to avoid ending up in the ferry channel, and just before or just after slack, since maximum-current times in Rich Passage present raging waters. Boat traffic is also a hazard in this narrow channel on busy days, so fly a flag and surface cautiously. The best ascent scenario here includes a swim toward the shallows near shore and an entertaining safety stop amid the kelp

Look for this *solitary piling, which is near the middle of the dive site.*

beds. A properly planned dive during slack current should be enjoyable by intermediate and advanced divers. The reef drops gradually, and divers can easily remain at their preferred depth and still have plenty to see by swimming parallel to the shoreline.

Location: Wautauga Beach is located on the Kitsap Peninsula between Point Glover and Middle Point in Rich Passage, just south of Bainbridge Island (see chart on page 52). Across the channel is Fort Ward State Park, and south of that, Orchard Rocks. A row of houses fronts the water from Point Glover south; not quite halfway down the row stands a single piling in the water in front of a house (currently blue), which sits at the apex of a very slight elbow along the shore. Anchor out from this piling at a depth of 30 feet and start your dive toward Point Glover. You'll see the reef after a short swim. Boat launches are at Fort Ward State Park on Bainbridge and at Illahee State Park to the north, on the west side of Port Orchard Passage. Air fills and dockside services are available in Bremerton and Seattle.

Sub-Sea Environment: A series of long rock spines that extend out from shore toward the middle of the channel and the sand and cobble-stones between them are the substrate for life on this reef. Scattered rocks and boulders offer additional habitat, as do the cracks and crevasses in the volcanic bedrock. Broadleaf kelp provides habitat for nudibranchs, snails, and kelp crabs. Rockfish, red rock crabs, and a diversity of brilliantly colored sea stars feed in and around the kelp beds, as schools of shiner perch and tube-snouts observe from above. Ling cod and cabezons roost amid plumose and rose anemones. As it descends, the bedrock eventually slips out of sight under a layer of cobblestones and broken shells. Many of the crevasses in the bedrock begin with a narrow yet visible opening and then extend beneath and under the spines. Peeking into these dark cavities with a flashlight often reveals surprising inhabitants. On clear days, sunlight penetrates to the upper portions of the reef and brings out the natural colors that one can only imagine when diving deeper with artificial light. The depth of the rock ribs runs to about 80 fsw, but the good visuals on this reef are in 15–70 fsw.

Sea Life:

Black rockfish	*Quillback rockfish*
Broadleaf kelp	*Red rock crabs*
Cabezons	*Rose anemones*
Giant barnacles	*Sculpins*
Kelp crabs	*Sea stars*
Ling cod	*Shiner perch*
Nudibranchs	*Snails*
Orange cucumbers	*Tube-snouts*
Plumose anemones	

Orchard Rocks
• CENTRAL PUGET SOUND •

Dive Type: Natural rock reef
Location: Rich Passage, south end of Bainbridge Island
Coordinates:
  Dive Site: 47-34-38 N
  122-32-58 W
  Manchester Boat Ramp: 47-33-21 N
  122-32-29 W
  Bremerton: 47-34-20 N
  122-37-20 W
Degree of Difficulty: All divers
Tricky Stuff: Current, approach, anchorage

Overview: Natural rock ledges, shelves, and ridges comprise this reef, which runs from the exposed rocks downward and outward toward the center of the channel. The rocks, kelp-covered near the surface, furnish habitat for the myriad and diverse sea life found here, and the rapid currents bring food as the tides flood and ebb through Rich Passage.

The Dive in Depth: All levels of divers will enjoy this dive. Although even stronger currents run farther north, the current can really rip through this portion of Rich Passage during a high exchange. At slack current, this can be a mellow underwater tour, and since the rocks run from the surface to the depths, you can easily pick your comfort level. The reef extends out into the ferry lane, so calculate your distance carefully, use your compass, and return to shallow water to make your ascent. Be sure to check the anchor set as you go down the anchor line, since the bottom is all rock here and minimum bite is available. Better yet, bring extra buddies on your visits to the Rich Passage dive sites and use a live boat pick-up system. Avoid surfacing beneath the fish pens to the south of the site and, of course, always display a diver-down flag.

Location: This reef is in the eastern portion of Rich Passage at the south end of Bainbridge Island, near Fort Ward State Park (see chart on page 61). Just north of the fish pens you will see a navigational marker on a pole atop exposed rocks. Anchor out from that marker in 30 to 40 fsw and descend on the anchor line. Boat launches are nearby at Fort Ward State Park and Illahee State Park. Another good launch site is to the south in the town of Manchester. Air fills and dockside services are available in Bremerton and Seattle.

Anchor out from *this navigational marker, descend, and follow the reef northward.*

Sub-Sea Environment: Volcanic bedrock—dropping, then leveling, then dropping again—forms a natural reef of barnacle-covered ledges. The shelves and crevasses support an interesting assortment of crawling, scooting, sliding, and swimming marine critters and act as a perfect little arena for the macro photographer who is looking for some eye-level, close-up pics. Giant barnacles, oodles of shrimp, and troupes of white sea urchins perform here, as do many crab species. Sea cucumbers are plentiful among the yellow coral. Alabaster nudibranchs, sea lemons, and sea stars add color and vividness to the gloomy substrate. Large schools of tube-snouts and shiner perch, moving as a single body, circle the reef as if accomplishing some important task, while the resident rockfish, sculpins, cabezons, and ling cod are left in charge of hanging out.

Sea Life:

Alabaster nudibranchs
Blennies
Cabezons
Corals
Decorator crabs
Giant barnacles
Giant sea cucumbers
Hermit crabs
Kelp crabs
Kelp greenlings
Ling cod
Orange sea cucumbers
Painted greenlings
Pile perch

Porcelain crabs
Red rock crabs
Rockfish
Sculpins
Sea lemons
Sea anemones
Sea stars
Shiner perch
Shrimp
Striped perch
Tube-snouts
White sea cucumbers
White sea urchins

DIVE

SITE

Orchard Point
• CENTRAL PUGET SOUND •

Dive Type: Artificial reef, concrete
Location: West entrance to Rich Passage, east of Bremerton
Coordinates:
  Dive Site: 47-33-57 N
  122-31-55 W
  Manchester Boat Ramp: 47-33-21 N
  122-32-29 W
  Bremerton: 47-34-20 N
  122-37-20 W
Degree of Difficulty: All divers
Tricky Stuff: Current

Overview: During World War II huge nets were placed across Rich Passage, from Orchard Point to Beans Point, to intercept any enemy submarines attempting to reach Bremerton from the East Passage. The nets are gone, but the concrete anchors for them are still in place and create an interesting underwater scene. This dive site, accessible only by boat, is fairly shallow and somewhat protected from currents, making it a good choice for a second dive after a deeper dive during slack.

The Dive in Depth: This dive site is suitable for all levels of divers. It's well out of the way of the ferries, and the bottom tapers off slowly, so depth is not a hazard for cautious divers. Even small-boat traffic is likely to stay clear due to visible rocks on the shore, but fly a dive flag anyway. Rich Passage is a high-current area, so although this site is out of the main flow, plan your dive for slack current when possible. If more than one buddy team is aboard, a live boat pick-up can be used during tidal exchanges.

Location: Orchard Point is at the south end of the eastern entrance into Rich Passage, south of Bainbridge Island. A small concrete abutment is visible on shore at the point, as is a small rock pyramid at low tide. Drop anchor in 25–30 feet of water and allow enough room for the boat to swing on the anchor line without going into the rocks. An imaginary line between this point and Beans Point on Bainbridge Island will put you on the submarine net anchors. A very good boat ramp is to the south in the town of Manchester. Bremerton and Port Orchard also have boat ramps. Air fills and dockside services are available in Bremerton to the west and Winslow to the north.

Sub-Sea Environment: Two massive concrete blocks, still joined by a long, rusty iron girder, loom underwater at depths of 40 to 60 feet. Lacking holes or crevices, marine life has taken hold on the tops and sides of the blocks and, where possible, slightly underneath them as well.

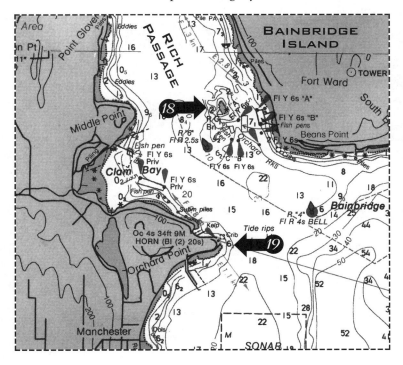

This lighthouse *marks Beans Point on Bainbridge. The net anchors are just around the corner, between Beans Point and Orchard Point.*

White plumose anemones and gumboot chitons cling to the concrete, while the sandy bottom supports geoducks, clams, rock and kelp crabs, and other assorted crustaceans. Frosted nudibranchs and clown nudibranchs prowl the nearby broadleaf kelp in search of snails and bryozoans. Ling cod, greenlings, and both black and China rockfish are commonly found at this site, and even a solitary dogfish may happen by. Flounders, sea pens, and giant sea cucumbers occupy the sandy sea floor around the anchor blocks. The sandy bottom drops off to scattered rocks as you swim east, and these rocks also offer an abundance of sea life.

Sea Life:

Black rockfish
Broadleaf kelp
Bryozoans
China rockfish
Clams
Clown nudibranchs
Dogfish
Flounders
Frosted nudibranchs
Geoducks
Giant sea cucumbers
Gumboot chitons
Kelp greenlings
Kelp crabs

Ling cod
Moon snails
Orange sea cucumbers
Painted greenlings
Pile perch
Ratfish
Rock crabs
Sea pens
Sea stars
Shrimp
Snails
Striped perch
White plumose anemones

DIVE

20

SITE

Blakely Rock
• Central Puget Sound •

Dive Type: Natural rock reef
Location: Southeast side of Bainbridge Island
Coordinates:
 Dive Site: 47-35-38 N
 122-28-49 W
 Manchester Ramp: 47-33-21 N
 122-32-29 W
 Eagle Harbor: 47-37-35 N
 122-30-25 W
Degree of Difficulty: All divers
Tricky Stuff: Anchorage

Overview: Diving "The Rock" is a multi-day adventure if you want to see it all. This vast basalt area creates a veritable scuba playground that surrounds the visible portion of Blakely Rock. Thousands of square yards of diveable reef provide a home for our underwater neighbors here and allow divers to choose their preferred depth for a sub-sea sightsee.

The Dive in Depth: All divers who are comfortable with boat diving should enjoy an underwater tour of Blakely Rock. Beware of the shallow portions of the reef as you approach by boat. Much of the bottom around this site is solid rock, so be sure to descend on the anchor line and check the bite of the anchor before beginning your exploration. Because of the shallow rocks around the reef, wise boaters generally give the reef a wide berth, reducing the threat of overhead boat traffic. Nevertheless, use caution during ascent, fly a dive flag, and leave at least a 50-foot safety rope attached to the transom. Reefs that rise to the surface like this one make 15-foot safety stops easy and enjoyable, and wise divers will afford themselves this opportunity.

Location: Finding a reef does not get much easier than this. Blakely Rock is located at the southeast end of Bainbridge Island, near the mouth of Blakely Harbor. Approach slowly and look for dive flags on any other boats in the vicinity. Use your depth sounder to avoid bottoming out.

If you lack marine electronics, drop anchor about a hundred feet from the rock and measure out the anchor line. In this scenario, try for a 30- to 40-foot bottom. Short-term moorage is available at Winslow, with restaurants nearby. Overnight moorage is limited, but if you call

Blakely Rock, *north of Restoration Point.*

ahead for reservations you might get lucky. Boat launches in Seattle are at the Armeni ramp in south Elliott Bay and the Shilshole ramp in north Elliott Bay. The town of Manchester, south of Bainbridge Island, also has a nice launch with plenty of parking. Air fills can be obtained at the dive shop at Winslow in Eagle Harbor, although it is a fairly long walk with your tanks, a little over a block from the public dock.

Sub-Sea Environment: As is typical of partially exposed natural rock reefs in Puget Sound, what you see above is what you get below. Bedrock, boulders, and pebbles join to make up this haven for sea life by forming craters, crevasses, crannies, and cubbyholes. Sea stars— sunflower, leather, blood, mottled, and ochre species—drape over the encrusted substrate, adding further color to the coral-painted backdrop. White, orange, and giant sea cucumbers contrast with the dark basalt as do the bright anemones and nudibranchs living on the reef. Broadleaf kelp abounds on the upper portions of the reef and affords shelter for a myriad of shy creatures. Acorn barnacles and rock scallops glue themselves to the rocks, ling cod come and go, and schools of perch cruise above the reef grazing on the succulent fish cuisine offered up by the tiny animals living here. Blakely Rock is a massive reef, and it's diveable on

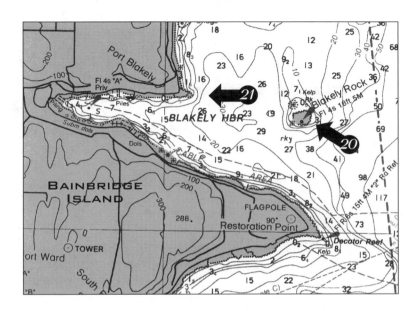

all sides. The north side is protected during ebb currents and gives way to a sandy bottom at intermediate depths; the south side offers a small wall with numerous holes and cracks to explore; and the east side drops as it runs a substantial distance out toward the East Passage. Bring a dive light to reveal the many marine creatures hiding in the hollows and crevasses, and plan at least a couple of return visits in order to explore the entire area.

Sea Life:

Acorn barnacles	*Giant sea cucumbers*	*Orange sea cucumbers*
Anemones	*Greenlings*	*Perch*
Black rockfish	*Grunt sculpins*	*Quillback rockfish*
Blood stars	*Leather stars*	*Red Irish lords*
Broadleaf kelp	*Ling cod*	*Rock scallops*
Buffalo sculpins	*Moon snails*	*Sunflower stars*
China rockfish	*Mottled stars*	*White sea cucumbers*
Chitons	*Nudibranchs*	
Crabs	*Ochre stars*	

Blakely Harbor, North Point
• C E N T R A L   P U G E T   S O U N D •

Dive Type: Natural rock reef
Location: Southeast side of Bainbridge Island
Coordinates:
  Dive Site: 47-35-80 N
  122-29-76 W
  Manchester Ramp: 47-33-21 N
  122-32-29 W
  Eagle Harbor: 47-37-35 N
  122-30-25 W
Degree of Difficulty: All divers
Tricky Stuff: Finding the octopus

Overview: This site consists of a series of natural rock fingers, extending down and out from the shore, separated by sandy bottom. Bedrock, boulders, and crevasses provide the terrain for the reef and the habitat for the marine life here. In fact, if you look closely at the rocky bluff on the north point of this harbor, you will get a good preview of the underwater scene you are about to encounter. Depending on which of the several fingers you choose to dive, your profile could be anywhere from 40 to 90 feet. Because of the area covered by these numerous underwater ridges, there is definitely more than one dive at this site. Remember your spot and return at another time to further explore the reefs.

The Dive in Depth: Boat traffic can be very heavy in this area. The reef is at the mouth of Port Blakely, just south of Eagle Harbor. Furthermore, both small boats and charter boats fish on the reef. Fly a dive flag, and use caution on your ascent. Much of the bottom is rock here, so

Blakely Harbor. *The dive site is east of this northern point of the harbor entrance.*

descend on the anchor line to inspect the bite of the anchor. Current is minimal at slack, and the depth along the sloping bottom increases gradually, so this is a good site for all levels of divers.

Location: This reef is located at the north tip of Blakely Harbor, at the southeast end of Bainbridge Island (see chart on page 65). Follow a compass reading of 30° out from the point about 150 yards and look for a depth of 50–60 feet on your depth sounder. If it appears you are on a line between the point and the Kingdome across the Sound, you are probably in a good spot to drop anchor. The other fingers of rock lie toward the channel from that point. Short-term moorage is available at Winslow, with restaurants nearby. Overnight moorage is limited, but if you call ahead for reservations you might get lucky. Boat launches in Seattle are at the Armeni ramp in south Elliott Bay and the Shilshole ramp in north Elliott Bay. The town of Manchester, south of Bainbridge Island, also has a nice launch with plenty of parking. Air fills can be obtained at the dive shop at Winslow in Eagle Harbor, although it is a walk of a little over a block from the public dock.

Sub-Sea Environment: This is a pleasant dive, with substantial life inhabiting the reef. The bedrock outcroppings create numerous small walls and ledges, and octopus dens can be found in the crevasses of the bedrock or under the boulders. Wolf eels live on the reef and broken clamshells scattered near a breach in the rocks will often disclose a hideout. A variety of sea stars beautify the reef with their brilliant colors. Black sea bass, quillback rockfish, and China rockfish linger near the silt-coated substrate, while the ling cod tend to rest in the surrounding sands and come onto the reef for meals. Striped perch, pile perch, shiner perch, and herring are plentiful. Because of the many crevasses and holes on the reef, a dive light is a must here to fully explore the locale and track down your favorite subtidal creatures.

Sea Life:

Black sea bass	*Pile perch*
Blood stars	*Quillback rockfish*
China rockfish	*Shiner perch*
Herring	*Striped perch*
Leather stars	*Sun stars*
Ling cod	*Sunflower stars*
Mottled stars	*Wolf eels*
Octopuses	

Alki Pipeline
• CENTRAL PUGET SOUND •

Dive Type: Artificial reef, concrete pipe
Location: Alki Point, West Seattle
Coordinates:
  Dive Site: 47-34-14 N
  122-25-56 W
  Armeni Ramp: 47-35-38 N
  122-22-54 W
Degree of Difficulty: All divers
Tricky Stuff: None

Overview: This splendid dive site is, well, ... a sewer. Sounds ugly, but this is one of the prettiest dive sites in Puget Sound. The sewer line, of course, has been inactive for many years, and marine life is so abundant that it is impossible to tell what forms the foundation of the reef until you see the gaping hole at the end of the pipeline and realize what you're looking at. This revelation does have a way of removing that brief consideration of actually swimming inside the pipe to discover whatever is inside. Because the reef is shallow, 15 to 35 feet, an almost Caribbean atmosphere overwhelms your vision on a sunny day. The long, narrow pipeline, easily accessible from either boat or shore, is a fabulous, easy-to-navigate night dive as well.

The Dive in Depth: Although small-boat traffic is likely to pass through the area, the biggest hazard is to become so enraptured by the beauty of this site that you forget to come up. Fortunately, the site is shallow and a tank of air goes a long way here, so explore and enjoy this dive until your buddy gets too cold to stay any longer. All levels of divers will enjoy the active and beautiful life-fest in progress on this reef.

Location: South of Alki Point a sizable row of boulders stretches out into the water. Just north of this large rock row is a smaller row, visible at high tide but more obvious at low tide. The pipeline runs west from this smaller row of rocks (see chart on page 73). At press time, there was an orange buoy near the end of and just slightly south of the pipeline. On a sunny day, the kelp line over the reef is visible from a boat at depths of 10 to 15 feet. Boat ramps are at the Armeni ramp in south Elliott Bay and at the Shilshole ramp in north Elliott Bay. Air fills and dockside services are available in Seattle.

Sub-Sea Environment: Dive this old sewer line on a sunny day with a camera, and your friends will believe your Tales of the South Pacific when you show them the pictures. Visibility is uncommonly good, the reef can usually be seen from the boat, and the multicolored kelp blanketing the old pipeline stands out dramatically from the surrounding tan sand. Enormous schools of tube-snouts linger an arm's

Shoreline east *of the Alki pipeline.*

length away, and squadrons of shiner and pile perch patrol the terrain just in front of wherever you happen to be swimming. A congregation of plumose anemones forms a massive pyramid at the open end of the pipe. Cabezons, sculpins, and rockfish rest here and there. Sea stars and corals, hydroids and sponges, jellyfish and chitons all help garnish the setting and bring astonishing colors to the reef. One would be remiss to explore the undersea world of Puget Sound and not dive this site.

Sea Life:

Anemones
Broadleaf kelp
Cabezons
Chitons
Corals
Cucumbers
Decorator crabs
Hydroids
Jellyfish
Kelp crabs
Kelp greenlings
Painted greenlings

Penpoint gunnels
Pile perch
Plumose anemones
Red rock crabs
Rockfish
Sculpins
Sea stars
Shiner perch
Sponges
Striped perch
Tube-snouts

Alki Reef
• CENTRAL PUGET SOUND •

Dive Type: Artificial reef, rock and concrete
Location: South of Alki Point, West Seattle
Coordinates:
  Dive Site: 47-33-27 N
  122-24-23 W
  Armeni Ramp: 47-35-38 N
  122-22-54 W
Degree of Difficulty: All divers
Tricky Stuff: None

Overview: This artificial reef, created by the state of Washington in an attempt to increase fish populations by providing habitat, is strewn about a vast area southeast of Alki Point. Numerous bargeloads of rocks and boulders have been dumped in several mammoth piles. The development of this reef is progressing well, and although it lacks the corals, hydroids, zoanthids, and other such colorful life native to the natural reefs in the Northwest, there is much to see. Current is minimal, and the dive is quite entertaining. *Note:* One diver recently recounted a dive story about this reef that included the presence of a six-gilled shark; no part of that story, however, will be discussed here.

The Dive in Depth: Boat traffic and fishing line are commonplace on fishing reefs, and divers should expect them on this one as well. It is possible to get deeper, but most of the reefs and marine life will be found in 50–75 feet of water. Plan your dive for slack current, fly a dive flag, and follow the usual precautions, and this will be an enjoyable site for all levels of divers.

Location: About 1.5 miles southeast of Alki Point, a Washington State fishing-reef buoy bobs around in 45 feet of water. The reef is broadcast both north and south of the buoy as well as beneath it. Boat ramps are to the north in Elliott Bay—the Armeni ramp at the south end and the Shils-hole ramp at the north end. Dockside services are available at Elliott Bay Marina. Air fills can be obtained in Seattle.

Sub-Sea Environment: Neighborhoods of plumose anemones impart a brilliant backdrop for schooling perch. Giant barnacles feed from their permanent homes upon the boulders, and the spaces between the rocks teem with

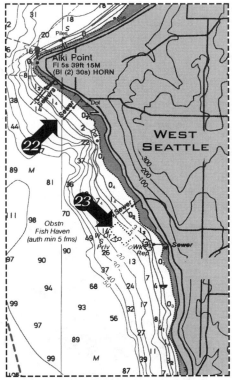

sea life. Giant and orange sea cucumbers are common here, as are the usual rock-reef inhabitants including rockfish, sea stars, and red rock crabs. Shrimp, blackeye gobies, decorator crabs, and sea urchins add variety to the reef and spice to the food chain. Nudibranchs ride on the undulating broadleaf kelp. Ling cod, cabezons, and ratfish rest on the sandy bottom or laze about on the boulders. Striped perch peck away at appetizing morsels on the encrusted rocks as mammoth schools of shiner perch move as a single body about the reef. Some of the boulder piles at this site are so massive that it's easy to spend an entire visit investigating a single pile and still not meet all of the inhabitants that populate this undersea abode. Reason enough, if one needs a reason, to buy another air fill and return to these West Seattle reefs for further exploration and contemplation.

Sea Life:

Black rockfish
Blackeye gobies
Broadleaf kelp
Cabezons
China rockfish
Decorator crabs
Giant barnacles
Giant sea cucumbers
Kelp greenlings
Leather stars
Ling cod
Mottled stars
Nudibranchs
Orange sea cucumbers
Plumose anemones
Quillback rockfish
Ratfish
Red rock crabs
Sculpins
Sea urchins
Shiner perch
Shrimp
Striped perch
Sunflower sea stars

This buoy marks *the artificial reef south of Alki Point.*

DIVE

SITE

Blake Island Reef
• CENTRAL PUGET SOUND •

Dive Type: Artificial reef, concrete
Location: Blake Island, west of Seattle
Coordinates:
   Dive Site: 47-31-48 N
   122-29-46 W
   Manchester Ramp: 47-33-21 N
   122-32-29 W
   Bremerton: 47-34-20 N
   122-37-20 W
Degree of Difficulty: All divers
Tricky Stuff: Calculating slack time

Overview: Massive concrete slabs with protruding rebar fragments have been dumped in disarray at the south end of this beautiful island, where they lie on a moderately sloping, sandy bottom. This site is one of several artificial reefs established by Washington State to enhance fish populations in Puget Sound. The reef becomes richer in marine life each year, and every dive here reveals inhabitants you didn't notice on previous visits. The site provides an ideal opportunity for active divers to make regular return trips in order to witness the development of a living reef over the years.

The Dive in Depth: At slack current, this dive is a reasonable choice for all levels of divers. The reef runs from 40 to 100 feet, allowing any diver to find much to explore at his or her depth of choice. During tidal exchanges, the current really rips along the south end of this island and the adjustments to the current tables are substantial, especially at slack

This buoy marks *the artificial reef south of Blake Island.*

before flood. Get to this site an hour before corrected slack, suit up, and watch the fishing buoy, mooring buoys, and flotsam to verify slack current. That way, you'll ensure a pleasurable dive, a controlled safety stop, and an easy surface swim back to the boat. As on any fishing reef, expect to encounter boat traffic and discarded fishing line.

Location: Blake Island lies just southeast of Rich Passage. A red-and-white Washington State fishing reef buoy is anchored over the reef near the southwest shore of the island, and two mooring buoys are positioned just east of that buoy. Drop anchor about halfway between the fishing buoy and the first mooring buoy in about 45 feet of water. Descend on the anchor line and swim south to find the reef, which runs east and west. There are a small marina and a restaurant on the north end of the island. The town of Manchester has a good boat ramp and is near the dive site. Boat launches in Seattle are the Shilshole ramp in north Elliott Bay and the Armeni ramp in south Elliott Bay. Air fills and dockside services are nearby in Bremerton and Seattle.

Sub-Sea Environment:
White and orange sea ane-
mones have found homes atop
the concrete slabs along with
sea stars, shrimp, and giant
barnacles. Orangey, rusting
rebar adds even more variety
to the pleasant hues con-
tributed by the nearby corals.
Flounders and sea pens live
on the sandy bottom and at
least one Pacific spiny lump-
sucker calls this reef home.
You'll see ling cod, kelp greenlings, ratfish, and many kinds
of perch and rockfish. Blennies and Christmas anemones
contribute to the constant
movement on the busy reef.
The random distribution of
the slabs has created many
large and small hidey-holes, and every one shelters some reef-dweller
that a flashlight will reveal to the careful observer.

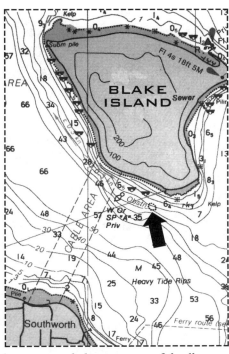

Sea Life:

Blennies	Pacific spiny lumpsucker
Christmas anemones	Pile perch
Corals	Ratfish
Decorator crabs	Red rock crabs
Flounders	Rockfish
Giant barnacles	Sea pens
Herring	Sea stars
Kelp greenlings	Shiner perch
Ling cod	Shrimp
Moon snails	Striped perch
Orange sea anemones	White sea anemones

KVI Tower
• CENTRAL PUGET SOUND •

Dive Type: Artificial reef, boulders and concrete
Location: Point Heyer, east side of Vashon Island
Coordinates:
    Dive Site: 47-25-22 N
    122-25-65 W
    Des Moines Marina: 47-24-12 N
    122-19-00 W
Degree of Difficulty: All divers
Tricky Stuff: Finding the sunken boat

Overview: Similar to other artificial reefs established throughout Puget Sound by the state of Washington as fish havens, this reef consists primarily of large boulder piles, concrete slabs, and long, hollow concrete pillars. The bottom slopes rapidly, and portions of the reef are as deep as 100 feet. A small cabin cruiser, covered with barnacles, lies near the reef in about 85 fsw. Divers visiting this reef should consider the Maury Island Quarry (Dive #27) or the sunken boat at Des Moines (Dive #26) as second-dive possibilities.

The Dive in Depth: This is an excellent site for divers of any level with a reasonable dive plan. It is not a high-current area, so the reef is diveable during an exchange, although planning to dive at slack will ensure an easy swim back to the boat. Diving at maximum current should be avoided; this is not a good drift-dive site, and discarded fishing line is ready to ensnare drifting divers. You are likely to encounter boat traffic (recreational and fishing), so display a dive flag. Toward the end of your dive, swim up some of the shallower rock piles and enjoy the brilliant colors from penetrating light on your way to a preplanned safety stop.

Location: Point Heyer is on the east side of Vashon Island, just north of Maury Island. The red-and-white KVI radio tower stands on the shore, and at press time, an orange-and-white Department of Fisheries buoy marked the reef. The debris is scattered across a broad area, and several dives are necessary to see the entire reef. The small sunken boat lies about 150 yards southwest of the buoy marker. Boat-launching facilities are at Des Moines Marina (which also has a fuel dock), at Redondo

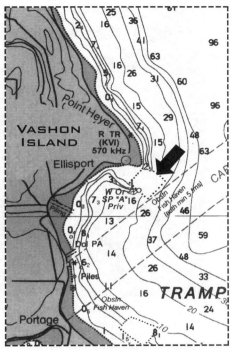

Beach, and on Vashon Island. Air fills can be obtained in Tacoma, Kent, and Federal Way.

Sub-Sea Environment: White and orange plumose anemones blanket the rock tops, adding light and color to the mostly gray substrate. Ling cod, kelp greenlings, painted greenlings, China rockfish, and many other fish seem to enjoy living on the reef. Herring and shiner perch travel in huge schools. Look for the broken shell piles that indicate the octopus dens, and bring your dive light to inspect the many holes and cracks among the debris. Rose anemones dwell on the bottom with the California sea cucumbers, snails, red rock crabs, and hermit crabs. The sunken boat lies at about 85 fsw, encased in barnacles. Nudibranchs slither across the kelp, while leather stars, mottled stars, sun stars, and sunflower stars drape themselves over rocks.

The artificial reef *is out from this tower on Point Heyer.*

Sea Life:

Barnacles	*Octopuses*
Blennies	*Painted greenlings*
California sea cucumbers	*Quillback rockfish*
China rockfish	*Red rock crabs*
Corals	*Rose anemones*
Hermit crabs	*Sculpins*
Herring	*Shiner perch*
Hydroids	*Snails*
Kelp	*Striped perch*
Kelp greenlings	*Sun stars*
Leather stars	*Sunflower stars*
Ling cod	*Tube worms*
Mottled stars	*White plumose anemones*
Nudibranchs	

South Puget Sound

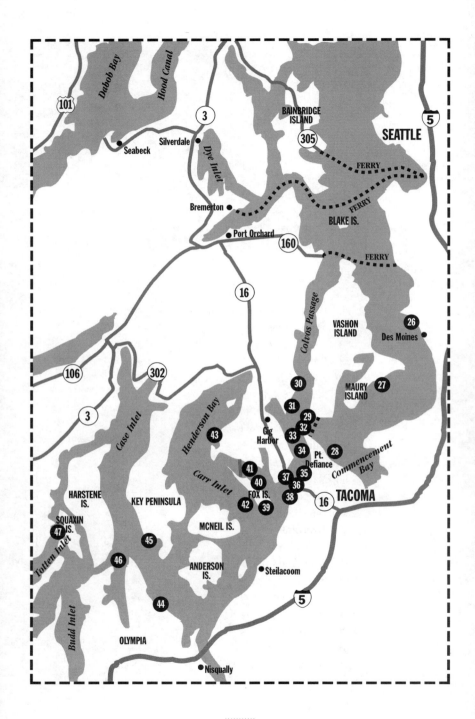

Des Moines Sunken Boat
• SOUTH PUGET SOUND •

Dive Type: Wreck dive
Location: Des Moines area
Coordinates:
  Dive Site: 47-24-64 N
  122-20-59 W
  Des Moines Marina: 47-24-12 N
  22-19-00 W
Degree of Difficulty: All divers
Tricky Stuff: None

Overview: Unless the barnacle-coated champagne bottles scattered about nearby are a clue, it is a mystery why this large pleasure craft rests at the bottom of Puget Sound. Because the superstructure of the boat is missing, one assumption may be that a fire destroyed her upper portions before she sank. This wreck appears to be about 50 feet long, sits upright in 55 fsw on an east–west line, and provides an interesting underwater tour.

The Dive in Depth: This is a fairly low-current area with a predictable bottom, so it's a good dive for all levels of divers. The bottom is sandy and affords

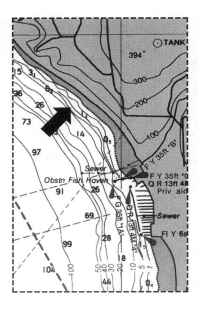

An obvious staircase

is visible on shore near   good anchorage. The wreck is shallow enough to
the sunken boat.   be a good second dive, perhaps after the KVI
Tower site (Dive #25) across the channel, and a
night dive here is fun too. Dive at slack when possible. If the current is running, the shore side of the wreck has the least current. Although the Des
Moines Marina is about three-quarters of a mile away, expect boat traffic.

Location: Less than a mile north of the Des Moines Marina, look
for a square, wooden, three-level staircase with a rock foundation. Go
out to a depth of 55 feet from here and continue north a short distance. A depth sounder or fishfinder should easily locate the wreck.
At this writing, there was a tire float attached to the wreck, but we
all know how those things seem to come and go. Divers who have
"seen the light" and acquired a small, inexpensive, handheld G.P.S.
can simply use the coordinates listed above to find the site. The nearest boat launch is at the Des Moines Marina, which also has a gas
dock, telephones, and restrooms. Air fills can be obtained in Tacoma,
Federal Way, and Kent.

Sub-Sea Environment: Bottom-paint manufacturers should shoot a commercial on this old gal. Barnacles are plastered across every square inch of the hull where the anti-invertebrate goo is missing, while the bright blue paint smeared on the substructure remains barnacle-free. Starfish are draped over the barnacles, and scalyhead sculpins graze on the encrusted railings. Rockfish have moved onto the developing reef along with the ever-present painted greenlings. Giant cucumbers, flounders, moon snails, and sea urchins inhabit the sandy-silty bottom, and a cabezon or two can sometimes be found. But it's the items left aboard the wreck that make this an interesting dive. Divers are strongly encouraged to leave everything as they found it so that others can appreciate the unusual assortment of everyday things that somehow seem oddly out of place in this setting. A rusty old circular saw sits in a box on the deck, along with various garden tools. Plastic milk crates lie in the sand, smothered with barnacles. Ropes, wires, and miscellaneous debris are visible through the hatches, as well as a tarp and what might be some old clothing. Please leave the junk where you found it—it looks much better where it is than it would taking up space on some table. Thanks!

Sea Life:

Barnacles
Cabezons
Flounders
Giant cucumbers
Moon snails

Painted greenlings
Rockfish
Scalyhead sculpins
Sea urchins
Starfish

Maury Island Barges
• S O U T H   P U G E T   S O U N D •

Dive Type: Sunken barges
Location: Maury Island
(south end of Vashon Island), Tacoma area
Coordinates:
   Dive Site: 47-21-79 N
   122-26-35 W
   Des Moines Marina: 47-24-12 N
   122-19-00 W
Degree of Difficulty: All divers
Tricky Stuff: Finding the sunken boat

Overview: Three wooden barges and a 38-foot pleasure craft lie in various stages of decomposition, in 40–70 fsw, off the south side of Maury Island. There is so much structure in such a small area here that it's sometimes hard to tell where one barge stops and another starts. The quarry that the barges served is no longer in use, but pilings and a conveyor loader still stand. The site is easy to find, diveable during low exchanges and teeming with marine life.

The Dive in Depth: This is a good site for all levels of divers. The sloping bottom continues to drop off past the barges, so stay aware of depth. Descend on the anchor line to make sure the anchor is not hung up on spiky barge parts where it will be difficult to retrieve. Fishing boats frequent this site, so watch for discarded fishing line and display a dive flag. Plan your dive for slack current at this site; the surface current is stronger than the bottom current, and surfacing down-current from your boat can present a difficult or impossible return swim. The pilings

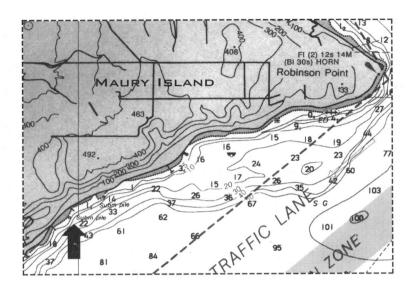

to the north of the reef receive good sunlight penetration and are covered with colorful anemones, sea stars, kelp crabs, and barnacles. Using these piling for your 3-minute safety stop will offer an engrossing distraction. Be aware of dangling gauges and other items that could get tangled on the many protrusions on the decaying barges, and swim far enough away from the structures to avoid damage to exposure suits.

Location: Maury Island is located at the south end of Vashon Island, northeast of Point Defiance and north of Commencement Bay. An obvious manmade cut chiseled into the top of the island is visible from a distance, and as you approach the island the pilings and the old conveyor loader are easily seen. Anchor off the west end of the pilings and begin your dive to the east, inspecting the two closest barges first. Continue east to find the third barge and the sunken boat. Boat launches are at Commencement Bay, Redondo, and Des Moines Marina. There are two nice ramps right behind Maury Island on Vashon Island, one at Burton County Park and the other at Dockton Park. Both have plenty of parking and restrooms. The nearest fuel dock is at the Des Moines Marina. Air fills are available in Tacoma, Kent, and Federal Way.

Sub-Sea Environment: The substrate, composed of sand, silt, and decaying wood particles, surrounds scattered rocks and broken shells. Flounders, tube worms, California sea cucumbers, anemones, and moon snails thrive on the sloping bottom among sea stars and hermit crabs. A giant octopus hides out under the barges and collects the local shellfish. The two barges between the first two sets of pilings at the west end of the reef are more broken up than the third, which rests farther to the east. The sunken boat is nearly straight out from the overhead conveyor, which is positioned in the center of the pilings. Sunlight does not penetrate to much of the site, so bring a dive light to help find the octopus.

Sea Life:

Anemones	Ling cod
California sea cucumbers	Moon snails
Flounders	Red rock crabs
Giant octopus	Sculpins
Hermit crabs	Sea stars
Kelp crabs	Tube worms

Three barges *and a sunken boat lie near the old quarry conveyer.*

Les Davis Reef
• S O U T H   P U G E T   S O U N D •

Dive Type: Artificial reef, concrete
Location: Commencement Bay, Tacoma
Coordinates:
  Dive Site: 47-17-10 N
  122-29-01 W
  Point Defiance Ramp: 47-18-20 N
  122-30-45 W
Degree of Difficulty: All divers
Tricky Stuff: None

Overview: A popular shore dive for local divers, this artificial reef is also easily approached by boat. As a shore dive, it requires a bit of a walk and a bit of a swim, but the reef is sizable, with little current, and is easy to find. Boat divers, of course, can simply drop anchor and slide down the anchor line, perhaps descending near one of the big ling cod likely to be lazing about on top of a large, hollow concrete slab. Either way, this artificial reef is worth a visit as its metamorphosis, which began right after the barge dumped the rubble and left the bay, continues from ugly pile of concrete to beautiful living reef.

The Dive in Depth: Currents are low through this area, and the varying depths allow all levels of divers to find the depths with which they are comfortable. Be careful not to venture too far east near the concrete fishing pier. Diving is not allowed there, and people fishing from the pier get upset when poor navigators straggle onto their portion of the reef. Since this site is a fishing reef by definition, expect boat traffic and possibly discarded tangles of fishing line. *A word of warning to new* *divers:* Although it is tempting to try to collect lost lures and weights on fishing reefs, the practice is best avoided. Rusty old hooks can cause infection or poke a hole in your BCD, and they are usually attached to discarded fishing line, which can easily become attached to you. The best decision is usually to leave them where you found them.

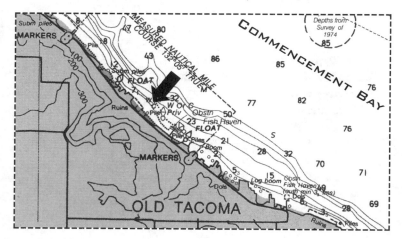

Location: Les Davis Reef is located on the southwest shore of Commencement Bay, across the bay from Browns Point. A concrete fishing pier is just east of the reef. As a shore dive, it is accessible from Ruston Way. When approaching by boat, watch your depth sounder at a depth of 50 feet, about 100 yards west of the concrete fishing pier. The depth of the reef is 30 to 80 feet. Several boat launches are in the Commencement Bay area, including ramps at Point Defiance and the Asarco ramp at the former site of the Asarco smelter. Totem Marina and Ole and Charlie's Marina both have launch slings. Totem and Point Defiance have fuel docks. Divers can get air tanks refilled in Tacoma.

Sub-Sea Environment: Created by the state of Washington to enhance fishing, this reef consists of a multiplicity of old concrete slabs that have been jettisoned to the seabed. A variety of sea stars, chitons, and blennies creep, crawl, and slither on the mishmash of slabs, which have also become a popular hangout for rockfish, ratfish, and schools of perch. Larger fish, including ling cod and cabezons, help populate the site, along with the smaller kelp greenlings and painted greenlings. Juvenile wolf eels have been encountered on the reef, and the sandy bottom is home to many flounders and crabs.

More than a dozen artificial reefs such as this one have been established in Puget Sound over the years, and all of them are interesting dive sites, although some have developed better than others. The Les Davis Reef is progressing well. Repeated dives on a site like this can help provide divers with insight on how a reef grows and an appreciation for the fragility of the underwater environment. Find a reef such as this one and plan at least one dive per year there—it is quite fascinating to observe the changes that take place over time.

Sea Life:

Blennies
Cabezons
Chitons
Crabs
Flounders
Kelp greenlings
Ling cod
Painted greenlings

Perch
Ratfish
Rockfish
Scallops
Sea stars
Shrimp
White plumose anemones
Wolf eels

Dalco Wall

• S O U T H   P U G E T   S O U N D •

Dive Type: Wall dive
Location: South end of Vashon Island, Tacoma area
Coordinates:
   Dive Site: 47-19-92 N
   122-31-11 W
   Gig Harbor: 47-19-55 N
   122-34-55 W
   Point Defiance: 47-18-20 N
   122-30-45 W
Degree of Difficulty: Advanced
Tricky Stuff: Depth, current

Overview: You have decided to assault the granddaddy of all walls in Puget Sound. It's slack before ebb; you roll over the gunwale and slip down to 50 feet, where you find the bottom and swim off to the south in search of the wall, observing the kelp beds along the way. You glimpse the edge, swim over, and look down. The calm and serenity you were feeling begin to slip away, and then one word comes to mind . . . YIKES!

The Dive in Depth: For advanced and experienced divers only, this site is not only deep but also in an area of very high current. It should never be attempted during a tidal exchange, since a strong waterfall effect (down current) can exist on the wall. Diving this site while any current is moving should be considered extremely dangerous. Dive at slack before ebb only, and do not enter the water until the current has stopped running. While a live boat scenario may be included in your dive plan, another good way to do this dive is to anchor on top of the shelf in about

The Dalco Wall *is easily located using this unusual house as a landmark.*

50 fsw, suit up just before predicted slack, and watch the wake behind the boat until it becomes minimal. Begin your dive when the wake is gone and the jellyfish are no longer cruising past your boat. With a boat fender handy, the boat tender can always attach the end to the anchor line, jetty the line, and make a live boat pick-up. The anchor will be easily retrievable after the divers are back on board and pick-up time will be minimal. The time frame on a live boat pick-up can become important if divers are drifting toward the Vashon ferry terminal.

Location: The Dalco Wall is located at the south end of Vashon Island, just east of Point Dalco and west of the ferry landing. Approaching the area from Point Dalco, look for a noticeable house on the shore with vertical, rafterlike deck supports. Just west of this house is a dilapidated shack with a concrete buffer wall at the shoreline. Anchor out from the concrete wall at a depth of 50 feet or less. A depth sounder will easily indicate the wall's location. Swim out to the wall and start your dive by touring to the east. Boat launches are at Point Defiance and Gig Harbor. Air fills are available in Tacoma.

Sub-Sea Environment: Diving the Dalco is serious business. It is

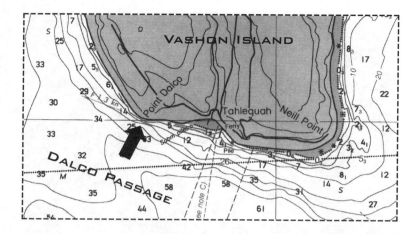

steep, it is deep, it is dark, and it can be dangerous. The wall begins in nearly 60 feet of water and drops virtually vertically to over 200 fsw. The wall is composed of sandstone-captured rocks covered with small barnacles. Straight down, visibility on the wall is usually about 15 feet and then everything goes black. Although fish are not overly abundant at this site, giant octopuses and wolf eels are both commonly seen. Quillback rockfish do hang out on the wall in places, and in the shallower water at the top of the wall, kelp greenling and an occasional small ling cod can be found. The engrossing experience of diving the Dalco Wall, however, comes from the structure and overwhelming mass of the wall itself. Small ledges and shelves break up the vertical symmetry, and undulations of the sheer cliff are noticeable, as are small cavelike openings in the sandstone. Bring a dive light to inspect these and to find the octopuses and wolf eels in their dens. As you ascend back to the top of the wall, enjoy the many life forms living on the reef above 50 feet, where sunlight penetrates to bring forth the colors of the marine plants and animals abiding there.

Sea Life:

Giant octopuses	*Quillback rockfish*
Kelp greenlings	*Striped perch*
Ling cod	*Wolf eels*

Point Richmond Minesweeper
• S O U T H   P U G E T   S O U N D •

Dive Type: Sunken ship
Location: Colvos Passage, north of Gig Harbor
Coordinates:
　Dive Site: 47-23-25 N
　122-32-92 W
　Gig Harbor: 47-19-55 N
　122-34-55 W
Degree of Difficulty: All divers
Tricky Stuff: Currents

Overview: This old wooden shipwreck is still worth a tank of air although it is well into an advanced state of decay. One reliable source theorizes that the 180-foot-long hull probably sank as a result of intentional neglect after her engine and drive train were removed. The ship's tanks and portions of the substructure remain and are now, together with tires, rotting timbers, and other debris, an interesting reef for divers to explore. Divers enjoying a two-tank day may want to visit this site after an earlier dive at Sunrise Beach (Dive #31) to the south.

The Dive in Depth: This site is in a high-current area and should be planned as a slack-current dive only. During slack current, this dive can be enjoyed by all levels of divers who are comfortable with boat diving. The sloping bottom continues to drop off to the east of the wreck, so stay aware of depth and elapsed time. When swimming near the discarded gill net that lies across the stern of the minesweeper, be careful to avoid entanglement and be conscious of dangling gauges or secondary regulators that might become ensnared by the net. Divers should always carry

This building *and the pilings north of Point Richmond help mark the wreck's location.*

a dive knife or dive scissors. Boat traffic is not usually high in this area, but keep an eye out for other dive boats and fly a flag.

Location: The Point Richmond minesweeper is located in Colvos Passage north of Gig Harbor. About one third of a mile north of the Point Richmond navigational beacon, five pilings on a north-south line are obvious near shore. This was formerly a marine construction yard, and a boarded-up building rests on blocks just behind the pilings. A depth sounder or fishfinder will clearly show the minesweeper about 150 feet out from the second piling from the north, at a depth of 60–75 fsw. The wreck can also be easily located by entering the water at the northernmost piling and swimming out toward the center of the line of pilings. This is a boat-only dive, since shore access is not available. A boat launch, a fuel dock, moorage, and restaurants are nearby in Gig Harbor. The nearest air fills are in Tacoma.

Sub-Sea Environment: White plumose anemones now decorate the top of the rotting hull of the minesweeper, which lies among boulders, cobblestones, tires, and wood particles on the sandy sea floor. An old fishing net is strewn across the disintegrating stern of the wooden vessel, where it supports spider crabs, snails, and other marine life while occasionally causing the death of diving birds and seals. Tube worms, glued to the sides of the wreck, wave their tentacles in the passing currents to collect their daily fare. Red rock crabs stow away in any opening they can find and stare out at passing divers. Ling cod, greenlings, and perch are common inhabitants of the reef. Sea squirts, sea urchins, sea cucumbers, sea pens, and sea stars all add color to the wreck,

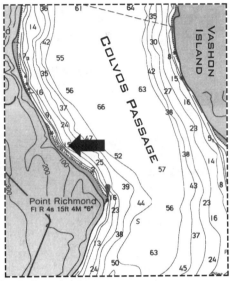

which lies parallel to the shoreline in 60–70 fsw. Swim to the pilings to the west at the end of your dive to examine the myriad sea life abounding on them and to turn a 3-minute safety stop into a pleasant and enlightening experience.

Sea Life:

China rockfish	*Sculpins*
Decorator crabs	*Sea cucumbers*
Hermit crabs	*Sea pens*
Herrings	*Sea squirts*
Kelp greenlings	*Sea stars*
Ling cod	*Sea urchins*
Moon snails	*Shiner perch*
Nudibranchs	*Snails*
Painted greenlings	*Spider crabs*
Pile perch	*Striped perch*
Quillback rockfish	*Tube worms*
Red rock crabs	*White plumose anemones*
Scallops	

DIVE

31

SITE

Sunrise Beach
• S O U T H   P U G E T   S O U N D •

Dive Type: Natural rock reef
Location: Colvos Passage, north of Gig Harbor
Coordinates:
  Dive Site: 47-21-84 N
  122-33-32 W
  Gig Harbor: 47-19-55 N
  122-34-55 W
  Point Defiance Ramp: 47-18-20 N
  122-30-45 W
Degree of Difficulty: Intermediate
Tricky Stuff: Currents

Overview: Although divers are long familiar with Sunrise Beach as a shore dive, approaching this site by boat eliminates a long and difficult trek to the shoreline, which is surrounded by private property, and an even more difficult climb back up the hill at the end of a dive. Over the years divers have interacted with the wolf eels on this reef, gradually gaining their confidence. Because the wolf eels are now accustomed to divers, this is an excellent location for aspiring photographers to get good pics of large marine creatures.

The Dive in Depth: Though this is not a deep dive—marine life is densest at 40–60 fsw—the currents here can be very strong and somewhat unpredictable. Divers visiting this site should be of intermediate skill or better, and dives should be conducted only during slack current. The best time is at slack before flood, which is about an hour and a half prior to slack before flood at Tacoma Narrows. Divers should always attempt this site as soon as the current goes slack and is swimmable, since currents during exchanges are too strong to swim against. Anchor at around 30 feet and descend on the anchor line to verify a good set on the rocky reef before swimming out to the ledges. Always fly a dive flag, since other dive boats commonly visit the area.

This gnarled tree *grows on shore near the north end of the Sunrise Wall.*

Location: Sunrise Beach is located north of Gig Harbor, near the southeast end of Colvos Passage. Several houses line the beach, with a bluff behind them. Look for a gnarled old evergreen tree on shore that leans out toward the water; begin your dive out from the tree and swim to the south to tour the reef. The site can be approached by land from Sunrise County Park by following the trail down to the shoreline. The closest boat launch is in Gig Harbor, and another nearby launch is at Point Defiance. Both launches have fuel docks and restrooms. Air fills are available in Tacoma.

Sub-Sea Environment: The substrate at this reef is volcanic rock, formed into small walls and ledges and eventually giving way to a sandy bottom. The entire starfish clan has declared this site its official reunion venue. Orange, white, and giant sea cucumbers also gather on the reef to find food in the rapid currents while adding brilliant color to the shadowy backdrop. The main attractions at Sunrise Beach, however, are the giant octopuses and the wolf eels. The octopuses can sometimes be found in the open during an evening dive; during the day, they can occasionally be coaxed from their dens by divers who offer food morsels.

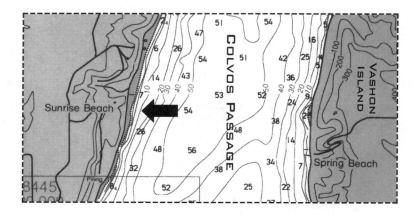

Adult and juvenile wolf eels live in holes and caves along the reef and are usually cooperative in accepting food from divers and mugging for photos. If you want to feed them, take a bag of squid or baitfish from a market or bait shop rather than grabbing resident crabs and urchins to sacrifice. Remember, wolf eels are wild animals, and there is really no reason for them to care one way or another about biting intruding fingers. Be cautious. Avoid rapid movements and resist the urge to handle or pet them. Be aware of buoyancy and fin position to avoid damaging the reef while ogling the eels. Other fish species living on the reef include striped perch, buffalo sculpins, flounders, ling cod, kelp greenlings, and painted greenlings. Tube worms and blennies live on the encrusted rock substrate, which is also colored with corals and sponges.

Sea Life:

Blennies	*Painted greenlings*
Buffalo sculpins	*Red rock crabs*
Corals	*Sea urchins*
Flounders	*Sponges*
Giant sea cucumbers	*Starfish*
Giant octopuses	*Striped perch*
Kelp greenlings	*Tube worms*
Ling cod	*White sea cucumbers*
Orange sea cucumbers	*Wolf eels*

Point Defiance North Wall
• SOUTH PUGET SOUND •

Dive Type: Wall dive
Location: Point Defiance, Tacoma area
Coordinates:
   Dive Site: 47-18-88 N
   122-32-46 W
   Narrows Marina: 47-14-77 N
   122-13-44 W
   Point Defiance Ramp: 47-18-20 N
   122-30-45 W
Degree of Difficulty: Advanced
Tricky Stuff: Currents, depth

Overview: Both sides of Point Defiance are blessed with great wall dives (see also Dive #33, Point Defiance West Wall). Both sites are packed with marine plant and animal life and have fabulous structure. One or the other is nearly always diveable in spite of the fact that only a short distance to the south the currents are raging under the Tacoma Narrows Bridge. The west side offers divers a vertical wall while the north side is a series of walls and ledges. Though sea life of all types abounds on the Point Defiance North Wall, this dive is worth doing for the structure alone.

The Dive in Depth: Fishing boats, fishing line, and fishers are the primary hazards at this site. The clay banks are a very popular salmon fishing area, and although the dive site here is closer to the shoreline than to the actual fishing area, anxious fishing boats who have drifted to the west end of the bank tend to accelerate rapidly back to the east end.

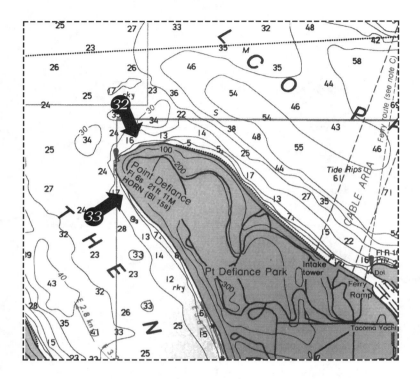

A live boat scenario is mandatory at this site. Under no circumstances should divers attempt a dive from an anchored boat at either of the Point Defiance sites. The live boat, with a clearly displayed dive flag, should remain positioned very near the dive team's bubbles to help ward off passing boats. Although this site is diveable during ebbing tidal exchanges, *do not* attempt a dive here during flooding currents. Dive at slack, during the early stages of ebb before slack, or during the early stages of ebb after slack, and expect the current to be running east to west, in reverse of the currents at the center of the channel. Plan to end your dive before reaching the west end of the wall to avoid being swept out into heavy currents and myriad boats. Depth is also a consideration for this advanced dive site; enter the water with preplanned time and depth limits.

   A word of caution: Colorful lures and bright red lead weights are cast into the water here by fishers to attract salmon. Unless the sole purpose of your dive is to recover lures and lead and you have come with the proper gear to do so, leave them alone. Not only do they have sharp hooks on them, they are also usually attached to heavy monofilament line, which can easily become attached to dive gear and create a serious entanglement situation. Be sure to carry a dive knife or dive scissors.

Location: This dive site is along the north side of Point Defiance. Approach the site during the latter period of ebb currents before slack or ebb, and the structures of current-carved clay on the shoreline will clearly indicate the clay banks below. Use a depth sounder to verify the location of the wall to avoid beginning your dive too far east and missing the wall altogether or getting caught by the swirling currents, which can push divers northward into the fishing boats. A navigational marker is clearly visible on the Point (see photo on page 106), and the reef is along the shore to the east of the marker. Point Defiance has a boat ramp and a fuel dock, but this popular launch gets very busy at times. Another option is the Narrows Marina, south of the Narrows Bridge behind Day Island. Air fills are available in Tacoma.

Sub-Sea Environment: The undersea walls surrounding Point Defiance are mostly clay, with a few embedded rocks and a little sandstone thrown in for diversity. Burrowing clams by the millions live in the walls and have created a spongelike surface with their syphon holes. Huge portions of the wall have succumbed to the constant burrowing and have broken off and fallen to the seabed, where giant octopus and wolf eels have remodeled them into comfortable dens. The clams then go back to work making the clay of the new wall resemble Swiss cheese. As you descend onto the reef, large schools of herring, candlefish, and shiner perch swirl atop the walls in a flurry of activity. Ling cod thrive on this reef, along with the usual rockfish, grunt sculpins, and greenlings. The walls give way to a sand-and-cobblestone bottom at anywhere from 70 to 90 fsw, where sea cucumbers, anemones, and other bottom dwellers make their homes. Various sea stars add color and variety to the reef, and substantial numbers of shrimp lend their quick, backward jump-starts to the busy atmosphere. As at any Northwest dive site, penetrating light does a poor job of illuminating under, around, and between boulders and hunks of clay, so take a dive light.

Sea Life:

Anemones
Blennies
Buffalo sculpins
Burrowing clams
Candlefish
Giant octopuses
Grunt sculpins
Herring
Kelp greenling
Ling cod
Mottled stars

Painted greenlings
Red Irish lords
Red rock crabs
Rockfish
Sea cucumbers
Shiner perch
Shrimp
Striped perch
Sun stars
Wolf eels

DIVE

33

SITE

Point Defiance West Wall
• S O U T H   P U G E T   S O U N D •

Dive Type: Wall dive
Location: Point Defiance, Tacoma area
Coordinates:
  Dive Site: 47-18-88 N
  122-32-86 W
  Narrows Marina: 47-14-77 N
  122-13-44 W
  Point Defiance Ramp: 47-18-20 N
  122-30-45 W
Degree of Difficulty: Advanced
Tricky Stuff: Currents, depth

Overview: A vertical clay wall with very small ledges drops 80 feet to a sandy bottom along the west side of Point Defiance. One of the true tall walls in Puget Sound, this site offers a comfortable, nearly slack dive during flood currents while water is raging across the north side of the point and on south through the Tacoma Narrows. Compared to many so-called wall dives in the Sound, this lofty wall is a monster—as are a few of its many inhabitants.

The Dive in Depth: Because of its depth, this site should be considered an advanced dive. Dozens of small boats whiz through the area on their way to drift and fish for salmon a little farther out on the clay banks as well as on the north side of the point. Watch also for wads of broken-off fishing line. Although it is best to plan to dive here during slack current, it is a comfortable dive during flood current. *Do not* plan a dive at this site during ebb currents! While the currents are flooding to the

105

Plan your dive *to exit the water before reaching this navigational marker at Point Defiance. Dive #32 is east of the marker; Dive #33 is to the south.*

south, the current near the wall runs in reverse, to the north. Enter the water far enough south to complete your dive and get back on the boat before you reach the navigational marker on the Point, or you may be swept out into strong currents and heavy boat traffic. A live boat scenario is mandatory at this site. Under no circumstances should divers attempt a dive from an anchored boat at either of the Point Defiance sites.

Location: This dive site is south of Point Defiance, on the west side (see chart on page 102). A navigational marker is evident on the point, and the wall begins about a hundred yards south of the marker. Enter the water even farther south and drift to the north if you are diving during flood currents. Allow enough distance to complete the dive and reboard the boat before you reach the navigational marker. The wall is long as well as tall, and missing the northern portion of it for safety's sake will still allow more than enough reef for one tank of air. To inspect the northern part of the wall, plan a second visit during slack current.

A boat launch and fuel dock are nearby at Point Defiance, next to the ferry landing. This launch is often crowded with salmon fishing boats; an alternative ramp is at the Narrows Marina just south of the Narrows Bridge, behind Day Island. Air fills are available in Tacoma.

Sub-Sea Environment: Because the substrate of the wall is clay, barnacles and anemones are not stuck to it in abundance as they are on some of the rock walls nearby in the south Sound. Mammoth octopuses and immense wolf eels, however, lodge on the reef and subsist on resident shellfish. Rough piddock clams burrow into the clay, causing portions of the walls to break off and contribute to the creation of the vertical structure of the site. Small sculpins pepper the ledges and the rocks along the bottom, where they are surrounded by colorful sea stars. Where there is rock, there are white plumose anemones adding luster to the realm with their gleaming tentacles. A peek inside an abandoned clam syphon hole reveals an occasional sailfin sculpin hanging sideways or upside down in the crannies or a suspicious quillback rockfish ready to defend its hideout from bubble-blowing intruders. Inspect the openings around the rocks on the bottom and along the ledges with a dive light to find the wolf eels and octopuses. Flounders laze about on the sandy bottom at the foot of the wall. Kelp beds near shore in the top 20 feet of water offer a diversity of marine life worth inspecting during a safety stop at the end of your visit.

Sea Life:

Flounders	*Sailfin sculpins*
Kelp	*Sculpins*
Octopuses	*Sea stars*
Quillback rockfish	*White plumose anemones*
Rough piddock clams	*Wolf eels*

Salmon Beach
• SOUTH PUGET SOUND •

Dive Type: Drift dive, junkyard
Location: East side of The Narrows, Tacoma area
Coordinates:
Dive Site: 47-17-83 N
122-32-98 W
Gig Harbor: 47-19-55 N
122-34-55 W
Narrows Marina: 47-14-77 N
122-13-44 W
Point Defiance Ramp: 47-18-20 N
122-30-45 W
Degree of Difficulty: Intermediate
Tricky Stuff: Current, buddy contact

Overview: Drift dives are exciting, relaxing, and—because you expend less energy and therefore consume less air—usually longer than slack-current dives. The reef along Salmon Beach is so scattered that drift diving is the only reasonable way to appreciate the junk jungle that composes it. While drift diving this site during tidal exchanges, it is possible to drift the entire length of Salmon Beach at a depth of 60 feet. If you are planning a two-tank day in south Puget Sound and you have only one shot at slack current, consider this drift dive as a nonslack alternative.

The Dive in Depth: While the depth remains consistent at any level down to 60 feet and the reverse current during flood is predictable, this dive should be considered intermediate to advanced, as should all drift dives. Practice good buddy contact while drifting this site, or hand-hold a 3-foot rope with your buddy to avoid the aggravation of buddy separation. Plan to dive at Salmon Beach during flood currents only, when the current in front of the houses runs north while the midchannel currents are running south. Be sure of current direction so that divers do not get caught in the heavy currents rushing south toward the Tacoma Narrows Bridge. See the Narrows Drift Dive, Dive #35, for information on drifting south toward the bridge. Boat traffic is heavy at times in this area because of salmon fishing on the clay banks at Point Defiance. Use a live boat, fly a dive flag, and stay close to the dive team.

Location: This is an easy site to locate without electronics. Salmon Beach is south of Point Defiance and north of the Tacoma Narrows Bridge, on the Tacoma side. A row of houses stand side by side right at the shoreline, and this dive site is straight out in front of the houses. Because the junk composing the dive site is scattered, the best way to dive the site is to drift the reverse currents, which run south to north, on the incoming (flood) tide. Certainly the site can be visited during slack currents but, as mentioned, the junk is widely scattered and a slack-current dive offers little entertainment. A live boat scenario must be

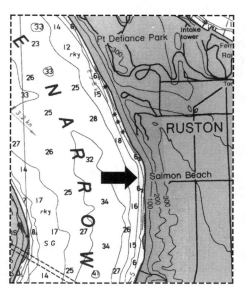

used, so drop divers off near shore at the southernmost house, then have them swim to 55–60 fsw and begin their drift dive to the north. If for some reason the current is not moving north at this point, do not enter the water. Try moving a little farther north up the row of houses to hit the reverse current. Nearby boat launches are at Point Defiance, Narrows Marina, and Gig Harbor. All three places have fuel docks, restrooms, and telephones. Air fills can be obtained in Tacoma.

Sub-Sea Environment: Ling cod? Sure, ling cod hang out here. Perch? Yep. Anemones, tube worms, and snails? They're right there on the bottom with the crabs and sculpins. Bull kelp and other seaweeds? All over the place. Starfish? Oh, about a million. Even great big schools of little dinky fish populate the panorama. It sounds like any other reef in Puget Sound...but that's where the similarity ends. Do this dive for the environment it presents. The beautiful white plumose anemones are living on an old wringer washing machine. The ling cod is resting next to the top of a wood-burning oven. The bottom portion of a pedal-driven grinding machine like the one Great-Uncle Ralph used to have in his yard has become home for tube worms and snails while serving as a nice hideout for red rock crabs and sculpins. A broken porcelain toilet bowl has oddly become a reef deserving serious contemplation since it now serves as a throne for a lazy red Irish lord. Hand tools, what's left of an early-model outboard motor, and the door from a Frigidaire icebox all lie, sheathed in barnacles, on the sand-and-cobblestone bottom. Even the kitchen sink is here...and it is fascinating. It is probably safe to presume that early residents of Salmon Beach made few trips to the dump yard. Certainly cause for justifiable lynching by today's standards, but the old junk has added interesting habitat and visual contrast to the reef. The diversity makes Salmon Beach a good drift dive, and if you tire of the artifacts, there are always the animals. Bring a dive light and expect the unexpected when you come to Salmon Beach: On one of our dives here, a little harbor seal joined us to pick up a few pointers on swimming technique and check out the latest in exposure suits.

Sea Life:

Anemones	Sculpins
Bull kelp	Snails
Crabs	Starfish
Ling cod	Striped perch
Perch	Tube worms
Red Irish lords	White plumose anemones
Red rock crabs	

Narrows Drift Dive
• SOUTH PUGET SOUND •

Dive Type: Drift dive
Location: East side of The Narrows, Tacoma area
Coordinates:
Dive Site: 47-16-84 N
122-31-99 W
Narrows Marina: 47-14-77 N
122-13-44 W
Point Defiance Ramp: 47-18-20 N
122-30-45 W
Degree of Difficulty: Intermediate
Tricky Stuff: Current, buddy contact, live boat

Overview: The entire shoreline here is a rocky slope, with a rock-and-cobblestone bottom and plenty of current. These features combine to create a perfect habitat for a variety of Puget Sound marine plants and animals. Although slack times at The Narrows are short, this dive can be planned for slack, which allows more time for further exploration of the interesting rocks, boulders, and dens that are plentiful at depths of 30 to 80 feet. Drifting the area, however, requires less exact planning for dive times and the opportunity to get an overview of a substantial portion of the site. To explore the entire area requires a return visit with—you guessed it—more tanks.

The Dive in Depth: Drifting this site just before or just after slack provides a relaxing dive while still allowing divers to control their motion if they want to investigate the seascape in more detail. Still, this is an intermediate dive and is not recommended for first-time drift divers

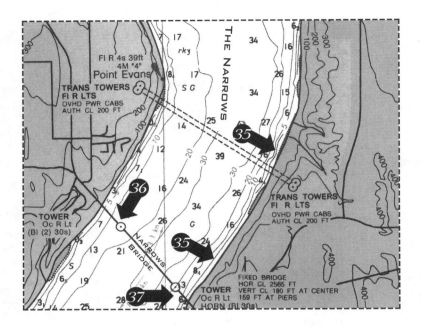

because of current strength and depth. The dive team should hand-hold a 3-foot rope to help eliminate the possibility of buddy separation, and the live boat operator should display a dive flag to alert boat traffic of diving activities in the area. Position the boat just west of and close to the drifting dive team to protect them from passing boats. If there is no depth sounder on the boat, begin your dive by swimming to shore and descending the rocky slope to the desired depth. If you plan your dive for slack current, you still must use a live boat scenario. Currents rage through the Tacoma Narrows channel; do not attempt to dive from an anchored boat anywhere in this region.

Location: This dive site is along the shoreline on the Tacoma side of The Narrows, just north of the Narrows Bridge. At flood current, try putting in a couple of hundred yards north of the power lines, and a 30-minute drift south should bring you up before you cross under the bridge, where currents increase. At ebb current, start at the bridge and drift north on a preplanned dive profile. Boat launches are nearby at the

Narrows Marina behind Day Island, which also has a gas dock, and at Point Defiance. Air fills can be obtained in Tacoma.

Sub-Sea Environment: Schools of candlefish and herring greet you at the surface as you enter the water and start your descent. A clutter of sculpins, including red Irish lords and buffalo sculpins, lie camouflaged along the ledges amid boulders, rocks, broken shells, and current-swept broadleaf kelp. Peering into the holes and dens as you drift along may bring you eye-to-eye with one of the many octopuses and wolf eels homesteading along the reef. Huge ling cod speculate on the edibility of the nearby rockfish, and perch and moon snails slip across the bottom. Look for giant acorn barnacles, kelp crabs, and sea cucumbers, as well as many sponges and hydroids. A 3-minute safety drift at 15 feet brings you back into the kelp-covered shallows penetrated by natural light and offers a colorful finale to your dive.

Sea Life:

Blennies
Broadleaf kelp
Buffalo sculpins
Candlefish
Giant acorn barnacles
Giant California cucumbers
Herring
Hydroids
Kelp crabs
Ling cod
Moon snails

Octopuses
Orange sea cucumbers
Perch
Red Irish lords
Red rock crabs
Rockfish
Sea stars
Sponges
Tube worms
Wolf eels

Narrows Bridge, West End
• S O U T H   P U G E T   S O U N D •

Dive Type: Artificial reef, bridge abutment
Location: West end of the Narrows Bridge, Tacoma area
Coordinates:
  Dive Site: 47-16-23 N
  122-33-28 W
  Narrows Marina: 47-14-77 N
  122-13-44 W
  Gig Harbor: 47-19-55 N
  122-34-55 W
  Point Defiance Ramp: 47-18-20 N
  122-30-45 W
Degree of Difficulty: Advanced
Tricky Stuff: Current, depth, boat traffic

Overview: A vertical wall with a predictable bottom depth, this is one of the signature dive sites of the Pacific Northwest. It is deep, it is dark, it is straight down, and currents are massive during tidal exchanges. This site is not for intermediate divers nor the faint of heart; but advanced divers with a good dive plan will find it exciting, colorful, and abounding with marine life. This dive, on the bridge stanchion on the Gig Harbor side of the channel, has a consistent depth all the way around the huge structure, but the support at the Tacoma end of the bridge drops off below recommended recreational limits on its west side.

The Dive in Depth: Dive sites around the Narrows Bridge are plentiful, but currents are rapid, and good dive planning is vital. Any diving under the bridge, whether near shore or elsewhere, should always involve

Colorful sculpins *are some of the most interesting fish in the sound.*

a live boat pickup for divers. Do not drop anchor, nor make any dive plan that includes an unattended boat. Published current predictions for the Narrows are for the center of the channel. Currents closer to shore can vary from those predicted slack times, and those slack times can be quite brief. The best method of diving this area is to arrive before predicted slack, suit up, and wait for the current wake at the stanchion to cease or slow to less than one-half knot. Entering the water at that point will provide adequate time for one team of divers to tour the site. Depending on the tidal exchange and bottom times, occasionally a second team of divers will be able to make the dive on the same slack after the first team surfaces, but some current will no doubt be encountered. In this case, make an ascent on the protected side of the stanchion. Always allow for a 3-minute safety stop at the end of your dive. Boat traffic is heavy on weekends and moderate on weekdays; fly a dive flag and keep the boat close to the dive area.

Location: This dive site is at the huge bridge support on the west end of the Tacoma Narrows Bridge (see chart on page 112). Boat launches are nearby at the Narrows Marina behind Day Island, at Point Defiance, and at Gig Harbor. Fuel is available at all three launches. The nearest air fills can be found in Tacoma.

Sub-Sea Environment: This octagonal bridge support is textured with giant barnacles from the waterline to the bottom, which lies at a depth of 118–125 feet. The east side of the stanchion is polka-dotted with white plumose anemones that have somehow managed to find moorage between the barnacles. Red Irish lords and other sculpins nestle between the barnacles and stare at divers, while tiny crabs tend to hang around upside-down and brandish their miniature pincers when caught in a dive-light beam. Countless sea stars sprawl about on the massive bridge support, and schools of striped perch attend at all levels, picking off their fare from the vast selection of smaller life on the reef. In summertime, a dive light is a necessity here, since depth and algae bloom can make it very dark at the bottom. Boulders, old lampposts, twisted iron, and other debris strewn about from the old bridge clutter the busy seascape at the base of the site, where you'll see bottom dwellers such as ling cod, giant octopuses, red rock crabs, and even giant nudibranchs. A short swim to the south of the bridge support, two 20-foot-square concrete anchor blocks rest in 120–130 fsw and provide additional habitat for marine creatures.

Sea Life:

Crabs	*Red rock crabs*
Giant octopuses	*Sculpins*
Giant barnacles	*Sea stars*
Giant nudibranchs	*Striped perch*
Ling cod	*White plumose anemones*
Red Irish lords	

Remains of Galloping Gertie
• SOUTH PUGET SOUND •

Dive Type: Artificial, bridge remnants
Location: East end of the Narrows Bridge, Tacoma area
Coordinates:
   Dive Site: 47-15-91 N
   122-32-80 W
   Narrows Marina: 47-14-77 N
   122-13-44 W
   Point Defiance Ramp: 47-18-20 N
   122-30-45 W
Degree of Difficulty: Advanced
Tricky Stuff: Current, depth, boat traffic

Overview: This is a great dive. Ominous blocks of concrete loom above as you bear witness to the site of an event that is a classic of Northwest history: The day in 1940 when the original Tacoma Narrows Bridge—ever since referred to as "Galloping Gertie"— buckled and collapsed during a windstorm and fell into the turbulent waters below. Although the dive is challenging because of depth and rapid currents with very short slack times, it offers abundant marine life and fulfills every curiosity that lured you into becoming a scuba diver. Anticipation fills you as you prepare to make your first dive here, and adrenaline rushes through your veins as you break the surface on ascent, already reliving an experience you will talk about for the rest of your life.

The Dive in Depth: This is an advanced dive, requiring a live boat and a capable skipper. Fly a dive flag to alert salmon fishing boats heading for the clay banks so that they can divert to the larger channel to the

A quillback rockfish *and a sculpin take shelter in the anemone-covered rocks.*

west. Current flies under the Narrows Bridge, and slack times are very short. Plan to arrive at the site 45 minutes before predicted slack, and *verify* that the current is running north (ebb) or south (flood) as per your expectations by looking at the water running past the bridge support. Start to suit up as you see the current speed decline, and enter the water when little or no visible wake remains at the bridge support. Managing to catch the last little bit of current moving one way and the first part of current moving the other way is about as much as you can expect. During that time, however, you will be able to swim freely in either direction and explore the site. This is a deep dive, and a 3-minute safety drift should be built into your dive plan.

Location: This site is under the Tacoma Narrows Bridge, on the east end, about halfway between the shore and the steel bridge support (see chart on page 112). Three of the bridge's anchor blocks lie just south of the present bridge in 80 feet of water, and at least two more rest just north of it. Portions of the old roadbed can be found to the east on your ascent up the rocky slope. Boat launches are nearby at Point Defiance to the north and Narrows Marina behind Day Island to the south. Both marinas have fuel docks. Air fills are available in Tacoma.

Sub-Sea Environment: The original Tacoma Narrows Bridge ("Galloping Gertie") went down to the bottom of Puget Sound during a major windstorm on December 7, 1940. The site lies under 80 feet of cold, dark salt water, and diving on the remains of Gertie brings vivid visions of the old gal twisting and romping in the wind before she gave way to nature's forces and plunged into the icy Narrows currents. Enormous concrete abutments, portions of the old roadbed, and debris and rubble galore litter the bottom between the shore and the current bridge stanchion on the east end of the Tacoma Narrows Bridge. Wolf eels, octopuses, sea bass, and huge ling cod patrol the area, while crabs and sea stars of all varieties reside on old Gertie's remains. Black rockfish and quillback rockfish are plentiful, as are schools of striped perch. But although the marine life here is plentiful and the dive itself is challenging, this dive signifies much more than plants and animals to most of us. To tour this site underwater, and then to stand and gaze at the existing bridge with our imaginations running rampant, brings about an understanding of loss and failure mixed with feelings of exhilaration.

Sea Life:

Black rockfish

Clams

Crabs

Giant acorn barnacles

Ling cod

Octopuses

Quillback rockfish

Sea stars

Sea bass

Striped perch

Wolf eels

Day Island Wall
• SOUTH PUGET SOUND •

Dive Type: Wall dive
Location: South of The Narrows, Tacoma area
Coordinates:
   Dive Site: 47-14-71 N
   122-33-84 W
   Narrows Marina: 47-14-77 N
   122-13-44 W
   Gig Harbor: 47-19-55 N
   122-34-55 W
   Point Defiance Ramp: 47-18-20 N
   122-30-45 W
Degree of Difficulty: Intermediate to advanced
Tricky Stuff: Currents

Overview: Just south of the Tacoma Narrows Bridge, swift currents rip along the shoreline, cutting ledges, shelves, and walls into the clay-and-sandstone substrates. The western side of Day Island (technically a peninsula today) juts out into this high-current area, where eons of tidal exchanges have carved out a wall that is now abundant with sea creatures. This interesting dive site deserves several return visits.

The Dive in Depth: This site should be considered an intermediate to advanced dive, not only because of its depth but because of the multiple currents, which can be running in several directions even during slack. This is a high-current area, and divers should carefully plan slack-current dives, with the understanding that some current will most likely still be running. Furthermore, opposing currents may exist on different

120

portions of the reef—that is, both north and south currents can be present, as well as current running away from shore to the west. At ebb, rip currents are also common at the south end of the reef. Use a live boat scenario when diving Day Island. It's OK to drop anchor, but have someone on the boat to toss off the anchor line on a buoy or fender, make a live pick-up, and then return to pull the anchor after divers are back

The Day Island Wall *is just out from this house.*

on board. At the base of the wall, the sandy bottom continues to drop off rapidly to depths that exceed recreational diving limits. Day Island also serves as a breakwater for two marinas, so display a dive flag.

Location: Day Island is south of the Tacoma Narrows Bridge on the Tacoma side of the channel. Toward the north end of the island, a row of houses lines the shore, one of which is a large pink house. Anchor out from this house in about 40 feet of water (a depth sounder will clearly show a rapid drop-off to indicate the reef location) and swim west to the wall. The closest boat launch is at the Narrows Marina, right behind Day Island on 19th Street. Other accessible boat launches include Point Defiance and Gig Harbor. All three have nearby gas docks. Air fills are available in Tacoma.

Sub-Sea Environment: Schools of shiner perch dart about on a diver-inspection tour as you descend from the top shelf, a depth of about 25 feet, down the face of the wall, which shelves out and down to a depth of roughly 70 feet. Broken shells left by the resident giant octopuses and wolf eels litter the ledges and offer clues to the den locations of these shy creatures. Buffalo sculpins and red Irish lords rest peacefully along the

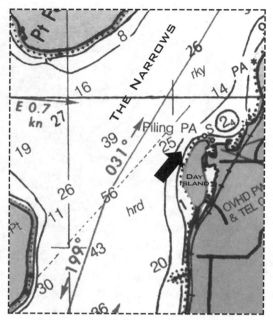

reef, awaiting the attentions of aspiring photographers who have become frustrated with trying to get a good octopus picture. The reef at Day Island Wall is over 80 yards long, and it supports a vast array of marine species from blennies to spider crabs. Visibility here is usually good by Puget Sound standards. The giant octopuses and wolf eels living on the wall have become accustomed to visiting divers and are not as skittish as those at some other sites. Feel free to enjoy, photograph, and admire them, but please do not harm them or try to take them from the reef. Their presence here makes this an exceptional dive site.

Sea Life:

Anemones	Red Irish lords
Blennies	Red rock crabs
Buffalo sculpins	Rockfish
Flounders	Sea stars
Giant acorn barnacles	Shiner perch
Giant octopuses	Shrimp
Kelp greenlings	Spider crabs
Ling cod	Striped perch
Moon snails	Wolf eels
Painted greenlings	

Toy Point
• SOUTH PUGET SOUND •

Dive Type: Wall dive
Location: Fox Island, southwest of Tacoma
Coordinates:
  Dive Site: 47-13-65 N
  122-35-49 W
  Narrows Marina: 47-14-77 N
  122-13-44 W
  Point Defiance Ramp: 47-18-20 N
  122-30-45 W
Degree of Difficulty: Intermediate
Tricky Stuff: Currents

Overview: This might be the place your mother warned you about as a kid. The first wall literally drops off from chest-deep water at low tide down to about 40 feet, where it ledges out a ways and then drops again to a depth of about 80 feet. The substrate is mostly sandstone and clay, with boulders lying about that have been set free by the current continually carving away the soft material that confined them. Also known as the Fox Island East Wall, this site is just south of the Tacoma Narrows Bridge, and currents are strong during tidal exchanges. As in most heavy-current areas, marine life is dense at Toy Point, and visibility is often quite good. Although this dive site can be reached from shore, approaching it by boat is much easier.

The Dive in Depth: The major hazard at this site is the rapidly sweeping currents present during tidal exchanges. A well-planned dive during slack current, however, will be excellent for experienced intermediate

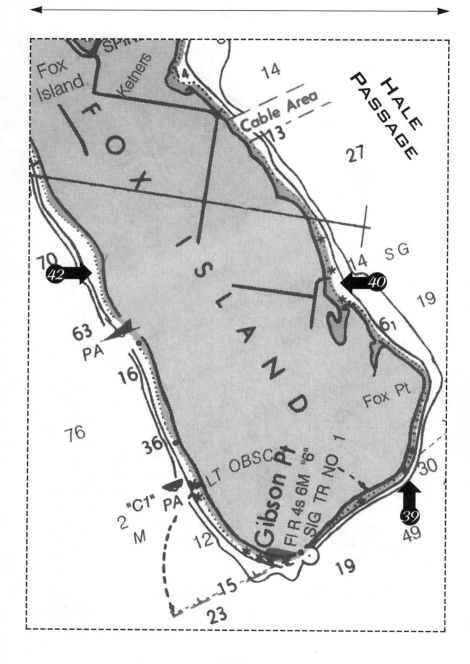

divers. A carefully drafted and executed dive plan may be conducted at this site from an anchored boat. However, a live boat scenario is more fun and eliminates the discomforts created by planning errors. Since inspection of the walls is likely to lead to a dive of 80 feet or so, plan a safety swim at 15 feet into your dive profile and treat yourself to a tour in the kelp beds along the top of the reef. Fly a flag!

Location: Toy Point is located at the east end of Fox Island in south Puget Sound. There are a navigational marker and light on the south-eastern point of the island (Gibson Point) with a small crescent shore-line just to the north. Farther north, the obvious rounded point with concrete pilings is Toy Point, and this dive site is just to the south of the pilings. Anchor far enough from shore to allow the boat to swing on the anchor line without grounding. Swim in toward shore to the top of the shelf and descend the upper wall to start your dive. Boat launches are at the Narrows Marina behind Day Island and at Point Defiance, both of which have fuel docks. The Narrows Marina also has boating supplies. The nearest air fills are in Tacoma.

Sub-Sea Environment: Beds of broadleaf kelp undulate at the top of the walls, camouflaging kelp crabs, nudibranchs, and snails. Several giant octopuses have made dens in the crevasses along the wall and under boulders. Colorful sculpins are sprinkled along the ledges and rocks, among shrimp, hermit crabs, gumboot chitons, and various sea stars. Corals and sponges add further decoration to the encrusted rocks. Hunters and fishers appear to have taken their toll on the Toy Point reef, but striped perch, quillback rockfish, ling cod, and kelp greenlings can still be found on the reef, although in small numbers.

While giant octopuses and wolf eels make any dive exciting, the structure of this site is itself intriguing and well worth close inspection during an underwater tour. The upper portions of this very colorful wall are given prominence by sunlight beams that penetrate the broadleaf kelp leaves and splatter brilliant rainbow hues across the reef. The deeper parts of the seascape reflect the work of eons of currents that have sculpted the soft sandstone and chiseled holes, caves, ledges, and small crevasses into the cliff walls.

These concrete pilings *mark the north end of the East Wall.*

Sea Life:

Blennies
Broadleaf kelp
Clams
Corals
Giant octopuses
Gumboot chitons
Hermit crabs
Kelp crabs
Kelp greenlings
Ling cod
Nudibranchs

Painted greenlings
Quillback rockfish
Red rock crabs
Sculpins
Sea stars
Shrimp
Snails
Sponges
Striped perch
Tube worms

Z's Reef
· SOUTH PUGET SOUND ·

Dive Type: Natural rock reef
Location: Fox Island, southwest of Tacoma
Coordinates:
  Dive Site: 47-14-61 N
  122-36-09 W
  Point Defiance Ramp: 47-18-20 N
  122-30-45 W
  Narrows Marina: 47-14-74 N
  122-13-44 W
Degree of Difficulty: All divers
Tricky Stuff: Current

Overview: Some of the best diving in south Puget Sound can be found around Fox Island. Z's Reef, located on the north side of the island, gets plenty of current during tidal exchanges and teems with current-loving marine plant and animal life. The reef is nearly 200 yards long, and most of it lies at depths of 40 to 60 feet. Because the shoreline is private property, this site is accessible only by boat.

The Dive in Depth: Plan this dive for slack current. Drifting this site simply does not allow time to investigate the octopus and wolf eel dens found on the reef, and furthermore, at maximum current the waters along this side of Fox Island are generally in high-speed mode. At slack, this is an exciting dive for all levels of divers. Slip down the anchor line to verify the set of the anchor on the rocky bottom, and ascend into the kelp-covered shallows at the end of your dive to check out all the little dinky critters living there. Arrange to have someone tending the boat in

Look for this *little shed on shore—it marks the west end of Z's Reef.*

case a live boat pickup is necessary, and display a dive flag since boat traffic in the area can be heavy at times.

Location: Z's Reef is located on the north side of Fox Island, just west of two small bays (see chart on page 124). The southern tip of Point Fosdick is across Hale Passage to the northwest. Look for some small off-shore boat docks and a little white building with two windows on the shore. The reef runs from that building to the east, where you will see a prominent house (brown at press time) built close to shore with a ter-raced yard behind it. Anywhere between these two landmarks you should be able to easily locate the reef at depths between 40 and 60 feet. Several other dive sites in this book are in the vicinity, including three more on Fox Island (see Dives #39, #41, and #42), and on a sunny day Mount Rainier stands proudly in the background, making this a superb area for a two-tank day with a lunch break. Boat launches are at the Narrows Marina behind Day Island, at Point Defiance, and in Tacoma. Air fills are available in Tacoma.

Sub-Sea Environment: Z's Reef consists of a series of ledges and shelves, small walls, and rocks. The depth of the reef varies from 15 to 75 feet, and if you swim the length of the site, you'll notice several changes in the formations. Several large octopuses live on the ledges under the rock outcroppings. These animals are becoming accustomed to divers infringing on their territory, and occasionally one can be coaxed out of its den for a tasty morsel. Wolf eels also inhabit the reef. Peer into the holes under and around the rocks with your dive light and you're likely to get the pleasure of meeting one. Large quillback rockfish are in attendance, as are schools of large striped perch. An assortment of colorful sea stars, including sunflower stars, sun stars, and mottled stars, adorn the reef. Ling cod, greenlings, and zillions of sculpins are common at this site, as are orange cucumbers, moon jellyfish, and a diversity of sea anemones. Marine life is so abundant and Z's Reef is so immense that it's a great reef to keep going back to. In all likelihood you will find your favorite sea creatures here sooner or later.

Sea Life:

Barnacles

Dungeness crabs

Kelp greenlings

Ling cod

Moon snails

Moon jellyfish

Mottled stars

Octopuses

Orange cucumbers

Painted greenlings

Quillback rockfish

Red rock crabs

Sculpins

Sea anemones

Shrimp

Striped perch

Sun stars

Sunflower stars

Wolf eels

Fox Island Bridge
• S O U T H   P U G E T   S O U N D •

Dive Type: Artificial reef, bridge abutments
Location: Fox Island, southwest of Tacoma
Coordinates:
  Dive Site: 47-16-65 N
  122-39-24 W
  Narrows Marina: 47-14-77 N
  122-13-44 W
  Point Defiance Ramp: 47-18-20 N
  122-30-45 W
Degree of Difficulty: Intermediate
Tricky Stuff: Currents

Overview: The bridges that link the islands of Puget Sound are usually built over the narrowest possible channels. These "narrows" of course have the fastest currents, and concrete structures in fast-moving salt water are naturally good dive sites. The Fox Island Bridge, on the north side of Fox Island, meets these requirements, and predictably, is a beautiful dive site, with unusually good visibility even during the dog days of August. It is accessible from shore as well as by boat. This site is a good choice for a second dive location after an earlier dive at one of the sites in the area that are not current dependent, such as the Point Defiance walls (Dives #32 and #33), Kopachuck State Park (Dive #43), or Fox Island West Wall (Dive #42).

The Dive in Depth: This is another south Puget Sound dive that must be planned for slack current. Strong currents rush under the bridge during tidal exchanges, and slack periods can be brief. A live boat

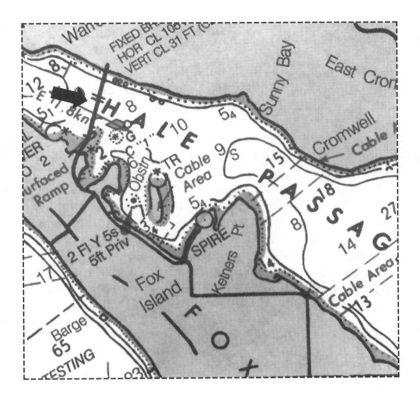

is a must. Diving from an unattended, anchored boat at this site is pure folly and should not be attempted. Boat traffic is very heavy through Hale Passage on weekends and holidays and moderately heavy on weekdays. Display a dive flag, and have the boat operator be prepared to warn away inattentive boaters. With proper dive planning, a live boat, and slack current, the Fox Island Bridge is recommended for experienced and intermediate divers.

Location: The Fox Island Bridge spans Hale Passage near the northwest end of the island. You can easily visit and inspect both rectangular center supports during the first half of a dive, and the neighboring supports to the north and south are easily accessible with a short swim and basic navigational skills. Boat launches are at the Fox Island ramp by the

Fox Island Bridge, Narrows Marina, Point Defiance, and Horsehead Bay. Air fills can be obtained in Tacoma.

Sub-Sea Environment: Above water, the two center bridge supports are larger than the others. Planted in 50–60 fsw, they are sheathed with plumose anemones from waterline to base, reflecting sunlight to brighten the site and improve the visibility. Monster barnacles lick their meals from the swiftly passing water, and quillback and China rockfish wait in suspension just off the pilings for enticing morsels to appear before darting in, hummingbird-like, to grab a meal. Decorator crabs cache themselves amidst the barnacles, while tiny sculpins nestle in to carry on their daily activities. Ratfish and dogfish are likely to swim by, and ling cod rest along the rocky bottom—sometimes curious, most times uninterested in passing divers. Sea stars move along the bottom and up and down the concrete supports. Old rusty metal framework and a rapidly rusting child's bicycle lie about near the foot of the pilings. Nudibranchs, sea pens, and flounders bring additional color and variety to the reef.

Sea Life:

China rockfish
Decorator crabs
Dogfish
Flounders
Giant barnacles
Ling cod
Nudibranchs
Plumose anemones

Quillback rockfish
Ratfish
Sculpins
Sea pens
Sea stars
Snails
Tube worms

Fox Island West Wall
• SOUTH PUGET SOUND •

Dive Type: Wall dive
Location: Fox Island, southwest of Tacoma
Coordinates:
  Dive Site: 47-14-34 N
  122-37-94 W
  Narrows Marina: 47-14-77 N
  122-13-44 W
  Point Defiance Ramp: 47-18-20 N
  122-30-45 W
Degree of Difficulty: All divers
Tricky Stuff: None

Overview: Despite its generally accepted name, the "West Wall" is actually located on the southern side of Fox Island. The site is accessible by boat or from shore and is situated in a fairly low-current area, making it a good site for less-experienced shore and boat divers as well as an excellent location for a second dive or a night dive. This dive is on a small wall, with the average depth of the reef between 50 and 60 feet. Marine life is plentiful, making a tour here both interesting and enjoyable.

The Dive in Depth: A dive along this wall is suitable for all levels of divers. This is a low-current area and is diveable during most exchanges. Still, planning dives for slack current is the best way to avoid a disappointing dive cancellation caused by currents, and visibility is generally better at slack before ebb. Display a dive flag, monitor the depth gauge, and make a 3-minute, 15-foot safety stop a part of

The West Wall *lies out from the dead-end street next to this house on the south side of Fox Island.*

your preplanned dive profile. Visibility can be poor during bloom cycles, so practice good buddy contact.

Location: As noted above, this dive is on the southern side of Fox Island, about midway up the island (see chart on page 124). From shore, enter the water at the end of Kamus Drive and swim south to the wall. To find the reef by boat, punch the coordinates into your G.P.S., or try the following: Head west along the southern shore of Fox Island until you start to see houses lined up along the beach. Watch for a road dropping down a slight hill perpendicular to the shoreline and you will notice the back side of a traffic barricade with driftwood piled up on the water side of it and the back of a diamond-shaped road sign. If you've found the right road, you will see a tall utility pole on the right side, with wires dropping to a much shorter pole on the left side of the road. Anchor due south in 40 feet of water and ride the anchor line down to start your dive to the south, where you will see the wall. Boat launches are in Tacoma, at Point Defiance, and at the Narrows Marina behind Day Island, which also has a gas dock. Air fills are available in Tacoma.

Sub-Sea Environment: The wolf eels living on this reef come to their den entrances to watch divers swim past and can sometimes be coaxed into coming out a bit for a taste of baitfish. Divers have worked hard to gain their confidence, so please respect them. With a dive light, you can also find octopus dens on this small wall. A few ling cod reside here, while buffalo sculpins and red Irish lords are plentiful. Painted greenlings and kelp greenlings are commonly seen from the kelp beds near the surface to the depths of the reef. Bottom dwellers such as flounders, giant sea cucumbers, moon snails, sand dollars, and blennies take their place at the base of the wall. Several species of sea stars creep up and down the walls, and shrimp populate the sandstone-and-rock ledges.

Sea Life:

Blennies
Blood stars
Buffalo sculpins
Flounders
Giant sea cucumbers
Hermit crabs
Kelp
Kelp greenlings
Ling cod
Moon snails
Mottled sea stars
Ochre stars

Octopuses
Painted greenlings
Red rock crabs
Red Irish lords
Sand dollars
Shiner perch
Shrimp
Spider crabs
Striped sea perch
Sun stars
Sunflower stars
Wolf eels

Kopachuck Reef
• S O U T H   P U G E T   S O U N D •

Dive Type: Artificial reef, tires and sunken barge
Location: Carr Inlet, southwest of Tacoma
Coordinates:
   Dive Site: 47-18-66 N
   122-41-39 W
   Narrows Marina: 47-14-77 N
   122-13-44 W
Degree of Difficulty: All divers
Tricky Stuff: None

Overview: With all the high-current areas in Puget Sound, it is nice to know about a few low-current sites that offer good visuals at shallow depths and have predictable bottom contours. Sites like Kopachuck State Park are confidence-builders for families, new divers, and new boat divers, and they also provide excellent night dives. The Kopachuck site is also a good choice for a second dive after a slack-current dive at one of the Fox Island sites (Dives #39, #40, #41, and #42), and it offers a variety of marine plants and animals. Because this site is in a low-current area, divers can dive here leaving an anchored, untended boat at the surface and still expect an easy return swim—even those who carry a compass but are not quite sure how to use it. This site is also accessible from shore.

The Dive in Depth: Carr Inlet is one of the few areas south of the Tacoma Narrows Bridge where current is weak, making this site suitable for all levels of divers. Fishing boats do frequent the site, so expect lost lures and discarded fishing line. Horsehead Bay to the south generates some small boat traffic, so display a dive flag and use caution on ascent.

Location: Kopachuck State Park is located on the east side of Carr Inlet and just north of Horsehead Bay, in south Puget Sound. Cutts Island, a tiny tree-covered island just north and west of the dive site, is the most obvious landmark in the area. A red-and-white can-type fishing buoy floats over the tire reef. Winds can blow either north or south in this inlet, so anchor on the leeward side of the buoy to avoid getting your anchor line tangled with the buoy line. Suit up after anchoring to allow time for sediment stirred up by the falling anchor to settle, thereby improving visibility during the dive. Descend on the anchor line and establish neutral buoyancy 6 to 8 feet from the bottom to begin your dive. To dive this site from shore, surface-swim out to the buoy from the state park, a distance of about 100 yards, and descend on the buoy line. There is a good boat ramp in Horsehead Bay, but parking is limited. Other ramps in the area include Fox Island near the bridge, Wollochet Bay, and Wauna, all with limited parking. Another option is to launch at the Narrows Marina behind Day Island and enjoy a longer boat ride to the site, with a great view on Mount Rainier on the way back. Air fills are available in Tacoma.

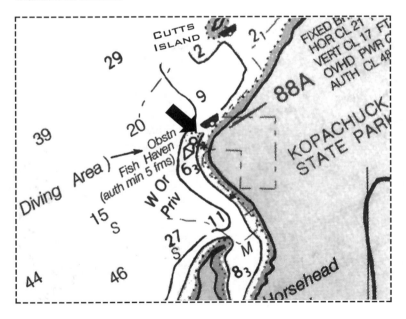

Sub-Sea Environment: This artificial reef consists of a sizable number of tires and a sunken barge at depths of 40 to 60 fsw. The tires are connected by ropes and the rope continues to the sunken barge, so everything is easy to find. Quillback rockfish hide out inside many of the tires, and numerous broken crab and clam shells imply that octopuses or wolf eels may live nearby and come onto the reef at night to feed. Striped perch are plentiful, and when not pecking at the encrusted tires, they like to follow divers and look for munchables in the silty soup stirred up by careless fin kicks. Shiner perch circuit the reef in enormous schools, moving as a single unit for the entertainment of divers who are aware enough to look toward the surface on occasion. Painted greenlings, pile perch, blennies, and kelp greenlings also inhabit the area. Red rock crabs rule the sandy bottom, scurrying this way and that with a pincerful of mussel or clam shell that is always coveted by one of their cousins. Various spider crabs, nudibranchs, and moon snails are also in evidence. Because the substrate is sand, take care to swim a little higher than normal and to kick your fins slowly and gently to keep from reducing visibility.

Sea Life:

Blennies

Clams

Crabs

Flounders

Hermit crabs

Kelp greenlings

Moon snails

Nudibranchs

Octopuses

Painted greenlings

Pile perch

Quillback rockfish

Red rock crabs

Shiner perch

Spider crabs

Striped perch

Wolf eels

Tolmie Barges
• SOUTH PUGET SOUND •

Dive Type: Sunken barges, tires
Location: Tolmie State Park, Nisqually Flats area
Coordinates:
  Dive Site (third barge): 47-07-46 N
  122-46-23 W
  (Red-and-White Buoys): 47-07-38 N
  122-46-17 W
  Johnson Point: 47-10-20 N
  122-48-90 W
Degree of Difficulty: All divers
Tricky Stuff: Finding the third barge

Overview: Although the Tolmie Barges have long been popular as a shore dive site, what most divers seem to remember most about diving here is the long, tiring surface swim. As a boat dive, the underwater tour here is relaxing, and air consumption is generally reduced, allowing you more time to inspect all three barges instead of just the two that are close together. The least-visited third barge is more nearly intact than either of the other two and offers more variety of structure. This site is not current-dependent and therefore makes a good choice for a second dive after a slack-current dive at Itsami Ledge (Dive #46). Divers new to boat diving might consider the Tolmie Barges site as well as the wreck at Taylor Bay site (Dive #45) to hone their boat-diving skills and practice getting a workable routine established for more challenging sites.

The Dive in Depth: With a depth of about 60 feet and very little current, this dive is recommended for all levels of divers. It offers learning divers good visuals in a fairly controlled environment, it's an excellent location for a second dive after an earlier deep dive, and it's a great choice for a boat night dive. Although current is light even during exchanges, good dive planning for non-drift dives includes calculation of slack current for water entry time. Swimming around any wreckage in scuba gear poses a potential problem of gear entanglement, so be sure to snug up dangling articles or swim far enough off the wreckage to eliminate that risk. Small boats do pass through this area, so display a dive flag.

Location: The Tolmie barges are located out from Tolmie State Park, just west of Nisqually Flats. For a shore dive, enter the water at the state park and swim out to the two red-and-white buoys to descend on the two close-together barges. The third barge is about 50 yards to the northwest, at a depth of 50–60 feet. For a boat dive, go to the coordinates for this third barge and drop anchor. From the anchor line, take a compass reading on the furthest red-and-white buoy so you'll know what course to swim to find the other two barges after a tour of number three. Boat launches are at Puget Marina just north of the dive site, Boston Harbor in Olympia, and Zittle's Marina near the tip of Johnson Point. Zittle's and Puget Marina both have fuel docks. Air fills are available in Olympia.

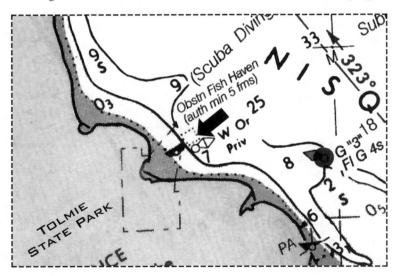

Sub-Sea Environment: Three sunken barges of decaying wood rest on a sand-and-silt substrate sprinkled with rotting wood particles and serve as a source of both food and lodging for fish, invertebrates, and seaweeds. Dozens of sunflower stars, mottled stars, blood stars, sun stars, and vermilion stars slither on and around the decomposing structures, adding color and brilliance to a rather dull backdrop. Tiny shrimp skitter backwards in retreat among the chitons and tube worms. Look for moon snails and nudibranchs as well as giant sea cucumbers. Quillback rockfish, red Irish lords, northern sculpins, painted greenlings, and ling cod are cooperative about posing for pictures. Striped perch swim among the wreckage, while geoducks, sea pens, and strawberry anemones dwell on the sandy bottom. The two barges that lie under the red-and-white buoys

Two buoys *are visible near the sunken barges.*

are surrounded by a sizable tire reef, which seems to go on and on and provides even more habitat for marine species. The barges themselves are interesting structures to explore and perusing all three of them in detail provides insight into underwater biodegradation.

Sea Life:

Blood stars
Broadleaf kelp
Chitons
Geoducks
Giant sea cucumbers
Ling cod
Moon snails
Mottled stars
Northern sculpins
Nudibranchs
Painted greenlings
Plumose anemones
Quillback rockfish

Red Irish lords
Red rock crabs
Sea pens
Shipworms
Shrimp
Snails
Strawberry anemones
Striped perch
Sun stars
Sunflower stars
Tube worms
Vermilion stars

Wreck at Taylor Bay
· SOUTH PUGET SOUND ·

Dive Type: Shipwreck
Location: Key Peninsula, north of Nisqually Flats
Coordinates:
    Dive Site: 47-11-13 N
    122-47-07 W
    Johnson Point: 47-10-20 N
    122-48-90 W
    Olympia: 47-02-75 N
    122-54-30 W
Degree of Difficulty: Intermediate during current;
    all divers at slack
Tricky Stuff: None

Overview: Just inside this small bay on the southwest end of Key Peninsula, the rotting hull of an old wooden ship almost a hundred feet long lies in repose on the sandy sea floor awaiting neoprene-suited visitors from above. Scuba diving on an old sunken ship for the first time is always a fascinating adventure as we examine the structure, view the living reef that has become a part of the wreck, and wonder about the chain of events that led to the ship's current state. The wreck at Taylor Bay is located in a low-current area, which means it is diveable almost anytime, but visibility can sometimes be poor. This site is an excellent choice as a second dive after a slack-current dive at Itsami Ledge (Dive #46) or Steamboat Island (Dive #47).

The Dive in Depth: Because this site is only slightly current dependent, it can be dived during nearly any tidal exchange. At slack

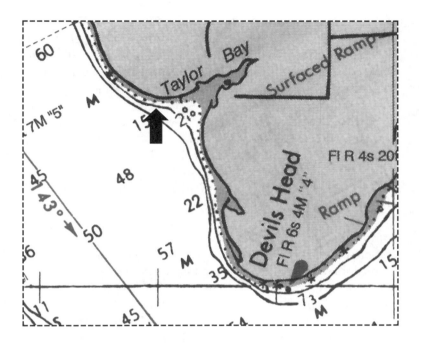

it is suitable for all levels of divers. If current is running, it is recommended for intermediate divers. The depth of the wreck is 40 to 60 feet on a sloping bottom, so depth is not a problem. As at all boat-dive sites, other boat traffic in the area is likely, so display a dive flag.

Location: This wreck is located just inside Taylor Bay at the southwest end of Key Peninsula, in south Puget Sound. As you approach the bay, watch for a dirt bluff on the north shore that tapers down to the shoreline on its west end. The wreck is directly out from the west end of the bluff in 40–60 fsw. There are no buoys on the wreck, but it can be easily located on a depth sounder or a fishfinder. If you do not have a depth sounder, look for a v-shaped cut in the bluff to the east of the taper, enter the water about halfway between the cut and the west end of the bluff, descend to 50 feet, and swim west to the wreck. Closest boat launches are at Zittle's Marina on Johnson Point and at Puget Marina and Luhr Beach southeast of that point. Air fills are available in Tacoma and Olympia.

Sub-Sea Environment: The sandy-silty bottom around the wreck is speckled with red rock crabs, giant California sea cucumbers, and clown and alabaster nudibranchs. Now in advanced stages of decay, the old wooden hull rests on a north-south line, perpendicular to the shore-line, and while all of the superstructure is gone, most of the substructure is to some degree intact. The wreck presents an engrossing opportunity for divers to scrutinize the shipbuilding talents of their ancestors and to view the biodegradation of the ship and the growth of a reef at the same time. The deck is overspread with a veil of white plumose anemones. Tube worms and barnacles are glued to the top and sides of the deck between the anemones, all of them waving frilly tentacles in search of nourishment. An array of sculpins live on the reef along with a few small and medium-sized ling cod. Schools of striped perch and shiner perch cruise gracefully over the hull, while several species of rockfish and the ever-present painted greenlings rest peacefully on the wasting timbers. Mottled sea stars, blood stars, and sun stars slither about on the wreck-age and along the sandy bottom, where they search for shellfish and add color to the drab substrate. To fully explore this site, bring a dive light. The ship sits upright, although listing on its keel, and you can see beneath it all the way around the wreck. In addition, numerous holes in the rotting hull tempt you to peer inside in search of marine creatures concealed by the darkness.

Sea Life:

Alabaster nudibranchs	*Painted greenlings*
Blood stars	*Red rock crabs*
Buffalo sculpins	*Rockfish*
Clown nudibranchs	*Shiner perch*
Gant California sea cucumbers	*Striped perch*
Grunt sculpins	*Sun stars*
Ling cod	*Tube worms*
Mottled stars	*White plumose anemones*
Northern sculpins	

Itsami Ledge
• SOUTH PUGET SOUND •

Dive Type: Artificial reef, rock and concrete
Location: Dana Passage, Olympia area
Coordinates:
    Dive Site: 47-16-52 N
    122-50-33 W
    Johnson Point: 47-10-20 N
    122-48-90 W
Degree of Difficulty: Intermediate
Tricky Stuff: Current

Overview: Over the years Washington State has established numerous artificial reefs in Puget Sound to serve as fish havens. The concept of enhancing bottom-fish populations by creating additional habitat has proven to be a good one, and nearly all of these artificial reefs have become beautiful dive sites. This reef, near the Itsami Ledge bell buoy, is highly scenic and supports a great deal of marine life. The rock mounds are widely scattered and offer enough variety to justify several return visits.

The Dive in Depth: This is a fishing reef, so boat traffic and discarded fishing line are likely to be plentiful here. In this high-current area, plan your visit during slack time and arrange to have an operator stay on an anchored boat. Better yet, use a live boat scenario in case a long, difficult surface swim or increasing currents pose a problem for ascending divers. The depth of the reef runs from 40 to 70 fsw along a flat, gently sloping bottom, and a properly planned dive should be a fun experience for intermediate divers. Display a dive flag.

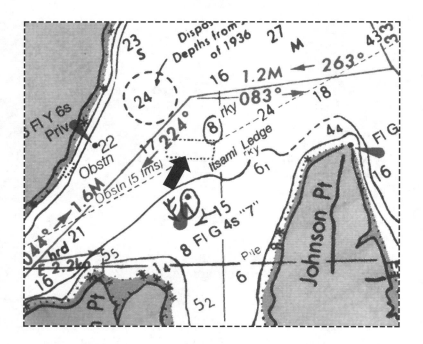

Location: Itsami Ledge artificial reef is located 1100 feet NNW of the navigational buoy at the east end of Dana Passage. There are no landmarks, since the reef is in the middle of the channel, but a boat equipped with a fishfinder or depth sounder should be able to pinpoint the rock piles by searching the bottom contour at the appropriate depth range. There are several boat launches nearby in Olympia. Zittle's Marina on Johnson Point also has launching facilities, a fuel dock, and restrooms. Air fills are obtainable in Olympia.

Sub-Sea Environment: Colossal concrete columns and bargeloads of boulders and rocks of all sizes have been discharged rather unceremoniously onto the floor of this South Puget Sound location. The heaps and mounds of rocky litter have adjusted nicely by dressing themselves with canopies of white plumose anemones and by enticing schools of perch to perform hourly swimming routines around them. Rockfish of all sizes add color to the big gray rock piles, with additional adornment being provided by red rock crabs, giant sea cucumbers, and seemingly luminescent nudibranchs. Orange sea pens have planted themselves in the portions of sandy bottom not showered with cobblestones, and anemones and tube worms blossom on the rocky reef. Prodigious ling cod patrol the on-site activities, their razor-sharp teeth glinting between slightly parted fish lips. Bring a dive light to penetrate the darkness of the many holes and crevasses amidst the rubble.

Sea Life:

Blood stars	*Red rock crabs*
Giant sea cucumbers	*Rockfish*
Leather stars	*Sea pens*
Ling cod	*Striped perch*
Moon snails	*Sun stars*
Mottled stars	*Sunflower stars*
Nudibranchs	*Tube worms*
Orange sea cucumbers	*White plumose anemones*
Pile perch	

Steamboat Island Wall
• SOUTH PUGET SOUND •

Dive Type: Natural, rock walls
Location: Squaxin Passage, north of Olympia
Coordinates:
   Dive Site: 47-11-27 N
   122-56-28 W
   Johnson Point: 47-10-20 N
   122-48-90 W
   Olympia: 47-02-75 N
   122-54-30 W
Degree of Difficulty: All divers, at slack
Tricky Stuff: Current

Overview: Though the muddy, silty bottom in the various inlets near Olympia limits the number of good dive sites in lower Puget Sound, this site offers an excellent dive on a series of interesting walls and ledges. Visibility is reasonably good because the rapidly moving currents keep the area swept clean of mud and silt. As elsewhere in Puget Sound, these same sweeping currents create a food-rich environment that supports a variety of marine plants and animals.

The Dive in Depth: Because it is close to the narrow channel of Squaxin Passage and the much larger Totten Inlet, currents are heavy at Steamboat Island. A dive properly planned for slack current, however, is enjoyable for all levels of divers. The best parts of the reef are between 20 and 70 feet, with the most interesting structure to be found in the shallower portions of that range. The presence of candlefish brings both salmon and salmon fishers to the area during exchanges, so some boats or discarded fishing line may be present. Fly a dive flag, dive at slack, monitor depth, and make a safety stop. Enjoy your dive!

Location: Steamboat Island is located at the west end of Squaxin Passage, north of Totten Inlet in south Puget Sound. The dive site is on the northeast side of the island. As you approach the north end of the island, you will see that the top portion has been coated with premix concrete. Besides adding to the island's "steamboat" appearance, the concrete makes an excellent landmark for the dive site, since the reef is straight out from the midpoint of this odd-looking cement coat. Anchor

out from shore in about 30 feet of water, and be sure to check the set of the anchor on your descent, since the volcanic rock holds some anchors almost too well and others not well enough. As you swim toward the north side of the island, the reef gives way to a sand-and-cobblestone bottom. Moving up to shallower water will bring you back to more walls and ledges, but be aware of changing current directions as you round the corner of the island. The nearest boat launches are at Arcadia and Boston Harbor. Zittle's Marina on Johnson Point has a boat launch and a fuel dock. Air fills are available in Olympia.

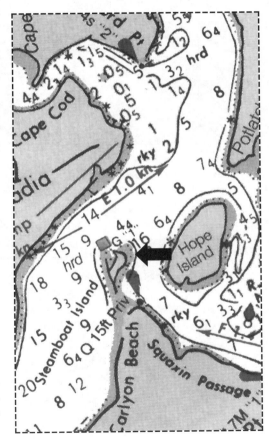

This house sits *at the north end of Steamboat Island.*

Sub-Sea Environment: The substrate at this site is volcanic rock and sandstone interspersed with cobblestones. Several terraced walls footed with current-carved ledges exist at various depths between 20 and 70 fsw. A resident dogfish with the confidence of a great white likes to greet divers visiting the reef to show off his sleek silver outfit and dignified swimming technique. Lazy ling cod lounge around the rocks, sating their appetites from the fishy fare passing by. Schools of pile perch and striped perch swim close the reef, while massive schools of candlefish and shiner perch swirl overhead. Remember to look up occasionally to witness the awesome beauty of large schools of small fish silhouetted against the penetrating sunlight. Enormous red rock crabs carve hideouts into the sandstone ledges, which eventually serve as habitats for other marine creatures. At least a googol of shrimp inhabit this site, skittering backwards as divers encroach upon their territory. Watch for brown rockfish, longfin sculpins, sea lemons, and moon snails. Cup corals and an assortment of anemones, tube worms, and hydroids are also common here. Sea stars sprawled across ledges or humped over unlucky shellfish add color and diversity to the interesting structure of this natural reef.

Sea Life:

Anemones
Blennies
Brown rockfish
Candlefish
Cup corals
Dogfish
Hydroids
Ling cod
Longfin sculpins

Moon snails
Pile perch
Red rock crabs
Sea lemons
Sea stars
Shiner perch
Shrimp
Striped perch
Tube worms

Hood Canal

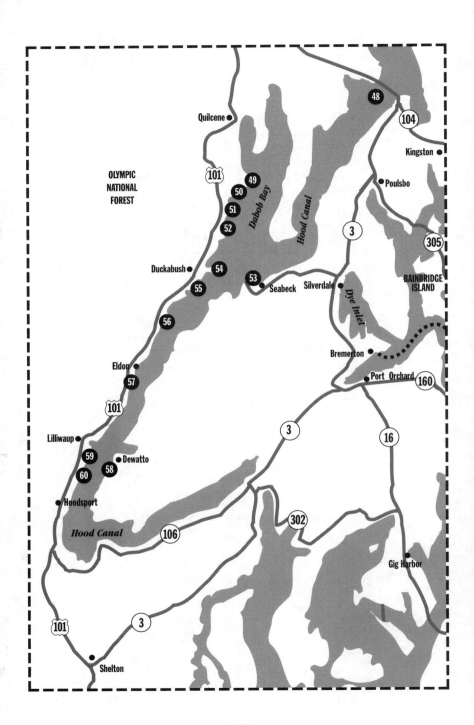

The Sisters
• HOOD CANAL •

Dive Type: Natural rock reef
Location: North Hood Canal, near Hood Canal Bridge
Coordinates:
   Dive Site: 47-51-50 N
   122-38-40 W
   Port Ludlow: 47-55-30 N
   122-40-80 W
Degree of Difficulty: Intermediate
Tricky Stuff: Approach, anchorage, current, boat traffic

Overview: This vast reef certainly deserves to be a multidive location on your must-do list. Two pyramidal pinnacles that break the surface during low tide spread down and out in all directions, creating thousands of square yards of natural rock reef. This is a picturesque site replete with fish, invertebrates, hydroids, corals, and sponges. Rock ledges, small walls, and myriad holes and crevices combine to form a superb dive site that is just south of the Hood Canal Bridge.

The Dive in Depth: Because of the distance from land, current, boat traffic, and potential depth, this should be considered an intermediate dive. The top of this reef is visible at lower tide and sports a navigational marker to alert boaters of the shallow rocks. However, the reef drops and spreads enough that there could well be overhead boat traffic when you are diving on the deeper portions, especially on the north side of the northern pinnacle. An ascent back up the rocks will provide a safe alternative to a direct ascent and will offer reference as well as good visuals during a safety stop. Because this spot is near the mouth of Hood Canal, there is more current here than at most other Hood Canal dive sites. Plan your dive for slack current, and always descend on the anchor line if leaving an untended boat, since the bottom is solid rock and good anchorage is important. Commercial harvesters of all types operate in Hood Canal; be sure to display a flag.

Location: Just south of the Hood Canal bridge, The Sisters protrude from the water in what appears to be the middle of the channel but is actually closer to the west side. The rocks are evident except at high tide, and the large navigational marker atop the southernmost pinnacle is easily seen. Anchoring in 30 to 40 feet should allow adequate space for the boat to swing on the line without going into the rocks, but do not enter the water until ample time has been allowed to observe a depth sounder after the boat has settled on the anchor. If you are new to the site, start by anchoring either to the north of the northern pinnacle or south of the navigational marker for your first exploration of the area. There is a good boat ramp, with restrooms, at Salisbury Point, just north of the bridge on the east end. Squamish Harbor also has a boat launch. Air fills are not available in the area, so take extra tanks if you are planning more than one dive. The nearest fuel dock is at Port Ludlow.

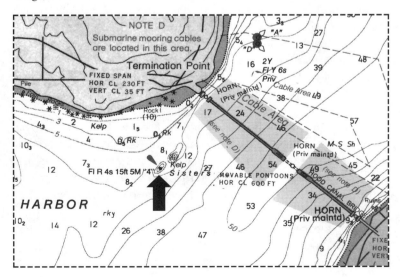

Sub-Sea Environment: The opportunity to dive The Sisters is reason enough to own a boat or to make friends with someone who does. The two pinnacles rise from a depth of 80 fsw to the surface, where they are blanketed by kelp beds. On this massive reef, there is no one particular place to dive—the entire area is a colorful dive site, with life abounding everywhere. Black rockfish, China rockfish, and quillbacks loiter near the rocky substrate like kids in a school hallway. Ling cod and cabezons live here and select their next meals from a smorgasbord of smaller animals. Sculpins of all sizes and colors repose on the encrusted rocks. Clown nudibranchs, frosted nudibranchs, Christmas anemones, and plumose anemones paint their dazzling colors on the reef, as do tall sea pens and a diversity of sea stars. Other inhabitants include calcareous tube worms, cup corals, zoanthids, and hydroids. Bring a camera, if you have one, to gather distinctive and vibrant pics. Even though the visibility can be quite good here at times, a dive light will help bring out many of the brilliant colors on the reef as well and illuminate the resplendent beauty tucked away in the subtidal dens and burrows.

Sea Life:

Black rockfish	Ling cod
Buffalo sculpins	Longfin sculpins
Cabezons	Plumose anemones
Calcareous tube worms	Quillbacks
China rockfish	Red Irish lords
Christmas anemones	Red rock crabs
Clown nudibranchs	Sea cucumbers
Corals	Sea pens
Cup corals	Sea stars
Decorator crabs	Shrimp
Frosted nudibranchs	Sponges
Hydroids	Striped perch
Kelp	Zoanthids

Pulali Point East Wall
• H O O D   C A N A L •

Dive Type: Wall dive
Location: North Hood Canal, Dabob Bay
Coordinates:
    Dive Site: 47-44-15 N
    122-51-21 W
    Seabeck Marina: 47-38-55 N
    122-49-75 W
    Scenic Beach Ramp: 47-39-30 N
    122-50-15 W
Degree of Difficulty: Intermediate
Tricky Stuff: Depth

Overview: Kelp-covered shallows, myriad rocks and boulders, and a tortuous underwater rock bluff with valleys and crevasses make up this site in north Hood Canal. The rocks and walls are silt-covered in this low-current area and thus lack many of the creatures found feeding in rapidly moving salt water. The structure, however, is astounding and, coupled with the respectable number of inhabitants, should place this site on the to-do list of any Pacific Northwest diver. This a long trip by boat or car for most of us, so you might want to enjoy a full day of underwater diversion by bringing an extra tank of air and making a second dive on the West Wall of Pulali (Dive #50) or at Quatsap Point (Dive #54) to the south after a lunch break.

The Dive in Depth: Current is minimal in Dabob Bay and the dive is interesting at all depths, making this a good site for all levels of divers. However, the reef drops off to well over 100 feet. New divers who are still

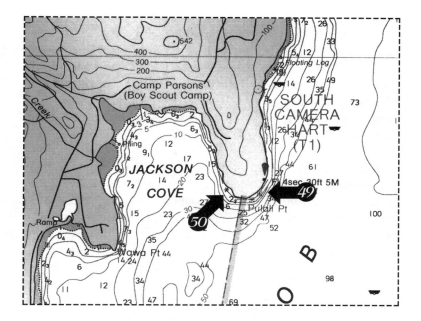

developing their buoyancy skills should delay their visit to the drop-off until they are confident of their abilities. The shallows above the wall run down to 40 fsw and are quite engrossing, decked out in myriad colors and packed with sea life. Novice divers who are comfortable with boat diving may wish to tour this area and try their skill at underwater photography. The shallow, kelp-covered rocks near shore also offer an excellent opportunity for deep divers to enjoy a swimming safety stop with great visuals during their ascent. Small-boat traffic is common in the area and some fishing takes place, so discarded monofilament line may be present.

Location: This site is located on the west side of Dabob Bay in Hood Canal. From the Sound, go around Foulweather Bluff, south under the Hood Canal Bridge, past the submarine station in Bangor, and west and then north around Taints Peninsula. Pulali Point will appear as a rock-bottomed bluff extending out into the bay northwest of Tsukutsko Point. This dive site is on the southeastern portion of that rock bluff. Anchor at 40 feet or so and follow the walls down to your desired depth. A good boat launch is just north of the site at Point Whitney. A better launch at low tide is at Quilcene, with restrooms available. On the east side of Hood Canal, Seabeck Marina has a boat sling that launches boats up to 20 feet, and Scenic Beach State Park just south of Seabeck offers a nice ramp. Air fills can be obtained at Hoodsport, but it is a long boat ride for air unless you've planned other dives for southern Hood Canal. Divers launching from Seabeck or Scenic Beach may want to get air fills in Bremerton, 15 miles east.

Sub-Sea Environment: Octopus! Several of these fascinating invertebrates dwell on this reef. You can easily find them by seeking out the broken crab and clam shells strewn about in the doorways of their dens. This silt-shrouded wall at Pulali Point is not a truly vertical wall but more of a rounded, rapidly descending bedrock, interrupted at intervals by small vertical walls, ledges, and loose rocks. White and orange plumose anemones, although not numerous, cast their shimmering white glow from rocks and boulders atop the wall. Sea cucumbers, red rock crabs, very large sunflower stars, and other members of the sea star family are common inhabitants at this site. Blennies and quillback rockfish join ling cod, cabezons, striped perch, and kelp greenlings in making up the fish population on the deeper portions of the reef, while shiner perch, tube-snouts, and small sculpins live in the shallows and feed on their favorite morsels in the broadleaf kelp. A little sunken rowboat rests in 110 feet of water, and a small ling cod often hangs out underneath it. Look for the octopuses in 50 to 70 feet of water—and be nice to them, just because.

Sea Life:
Blennies
Broadleaf kelp
Cabezons
Kelp greenlings
Ling cod
Octopuses
Orange plumose anemones
Quillback rockfish
Red rock crabs

Sculpins
Sea cucumbers
Sea stars
Shiner perch
Striped perch
Sunflower stars
Tube-snouts
White plumose anemones

DIVE

50

SITE

Pulali Point West Wall and South Tip
• HOOD CANAL •

Dive Type: Wall dive
Location: North Hood Canal, Dabob Bay
Coordinates:
    Dive Site: 47-44-18 N
    122-51-58 W
    Seabeck Marina: 47-38-55 N
    122-49-75 W
    Scenic Beach Ramp: 47-39-30 N
    122-50-15 W
Degree of Difficulty: West Wall intermediate to advanced;
    southern tip all divers
Tricky Stuff: Depth

Overview: There is so much rock structure at Pulali Point that you'll need several return trips to observe all of this immense seascape. Some divers prefer the meandering rock walls on the east side of the point (Dive #49), some prefer the small walls and broken rocks off the southern tip of the point near Jackson Cove, and still others like to investigate the deep wall on the west side of Pulali inside Jackson Cove. This description covers the west wall and the south tip of Pulali Point. However, although we've treated them as one dive site, it would be impossible to tour both on one tank of air unless you're one of the elite few diving with a rebreather. Those of us who have yet to win the Lotto would do well to plan an entire dive day at Pulali, with two or even three tanks of air, to fully appreciate this vast area.

The Dive in Depth: The West Wall is an intermediate to advanced dive because of depth, while the southern tip and the remainder of the reef are suitable for all levels of divers. Currents are minimal in this part of Hood Canal, and diving from an anchored boat presents no problems unless winds are strong. Slip down the anchor line on the way to the reef to inspect the bite of the anchor, since much of the seabed is solid rock,

and display a diver-down flag on the boat. Preplan your dive profile on the deep wall, and allow for a shallow safety stop in the colorful kelp beds at the end of your sub-sea tour.

Location: As you approach the Jackson Cove side of Pulali Point by boat, a sizable rock pinnacle is obvious near shore, with a tiny crescent beach adjacent to it on the northwest side (see chart on page 159). Anchor out from the juncture of the rock and the beach and swim out

Nudibranches *are some of the most beautiful creatures found on the reef,*

at a compass heading of 240° to locate the top of the West Wall at a depth of 60 fsw. After touring the wall, swim to the east to find the smaller walls and broken rock in 20–70 fsw. One boat launch is north of the site at Point Whitney, and another is across the Canal at Scenic Beach State Park. Seabeck Marina has a boat sling to launch boats up to 20 feet in length and a gas dock. From the east side of the Canal, the nearest air fills are in Bremerton; on the west side, air fills are to the south at Potlatch.

Sub-Sea Environment: The deep West Wall begins at a depth of 60 fsw and drops precipitously to a 120 fsw cleft, with fissures and crevasses. Although looking at colorless, silt-covered rocks can become humdrum at some Hood Canal sites, a tour down the West Wall is rescued from tedium by the giant octopuses concealed in the gaping cracks. The lustrous sheen cast by communities of plumose anemones, and the constant movement of passing fish, fleeing shrimp, and scurrying crabs also help alleviate the potential monotony of the gray substrate. Black rockfish, copper rockfish, and quillback rockfish attend the wall, intermittently stalked by toothy ling cod. A swim to the east, after ascending to the top of the wall, brings divers toward the southern tip of the Point, where small walls and broken rocks compose shallower, more densely populated reefs before giving way to a sandy bottom. Marine life on these segments of the reef includes flounders, blackeye gobies, greenlings, and perch, as well as several species of crab. Credit for lightening, brightening, and decorating the gloomy backdrop goes to nudibranchs, sea stars, tube worms, and sea cucumbers, as well as multicolored kelp.

Sea Life:

Black rockfish
Blackeye gobies
Broadleaf kelp
Copper rockfish
Decorator crabs
Dungeness crabs
Flounders
Giant octopuses
Giant sea cucumbers
Hermit crabs
Kelp greenlings
Kelp crabs
Ling cod

Nudibranchs
Orange sea cucumbers
Painted greenlings
Pile perch
Plumose anemones
Quillback rockfish
Red rock crabs
Sea stars
Shiner perch
Shrimp
Striped perch
Tube worms

Sea Mount (The Pinnacle)
• HOOD CANAL •

Dive Type: Natural rock reef
Location: Northern Hood Canal, Dabob Bay
Coordinates:
   Dive Site: 47-43-45 N
   122-52-50 W
   Seabeck Marina: 47-38-55 N
   122-49-75 W
   Scenic Beach State Park: 47-39-30 N
   122-50-15 W
Degree of Difficulty: All divers
Tricky Stuff: Finding a landmark

Overview: This natural reef, shaped roughly like a truncated cone, rises from the depths of Hood Canal to within 30 feet of the surface, where it culminates in a flat summit approximately 60 by 30 feet. This is an excellent site for a multilevel dive: start atop the summit, descend to your preplanned depth, and tour the pinnacle on a circular swim back to the top. Make the most of your time in the area by planning an earlier or later dive at one of the other nearby sites in northern Hood Canal described in this book.

The Dive in Depth: This is a wonderful dive for all levels of divers. Current is minimal, and marine life is abundant. Let out plenty of anchor line and slip down the rope when entering the water to ensure a good set of the anchor before starting your dive. Although the mount provides plenty of good anchorage, the top of the pinnacle is not all that large, and if winds are blowing hard enough to cause the anchor to pull

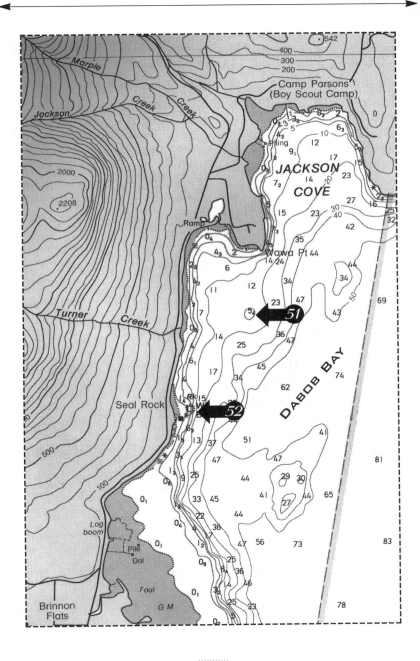

out, the boat is likely to be gone when divers surface, since the bottom around the pinnacle will probably be too deep for the anchor to reach.

New divers will be comfortable in their preferred depth range, with lots to see and no vertical drop-offs to challenge their buoyancy control. Advanced divers can likewise dive to their preferred depth range and search the many large holes and cavities in the reef for a peek at the sea bass, or the giant octopuses. Finishing your dive atop the pinnacle permits a longer dive experience, close proximity to the boat, and easy access to the anchor line for those who prefer a reference point while they are ascending. Display a dive flag, since fishing boats do frequent the reef in search of bottom fish. As always, listen and watch for boat traffic during ascent, and expect fishing line on and around the reef.

Location: This reef is located in Dabob Bay, in northern Hood Canal, 4.3 miles north of Pleasant Harbor and just south of Wawa Point (see chart on page 165). Sea Mount is a substantial distance from shore, so landmark identification for this location is difficult. The reef can be easily located with a G.P.S. using the coordinates above. Divers without G.P.S. equipment can try navigating due south from the eastern edge of Wawa Point for about a third of a mile while using a depth sounder. The pinnacle rises from 100+ fsw to 30 fsw. Everywhere else in the immediate area is deep, so if a depth of 80 feet or less is recorded, begin circling to locate the top of the mount. A boat launch inside Wawa Point is usable at high tide; a better one is to the north at Point Whitney. Scenic Beach State Park and Seabeck Marina, both across the Canal to the southeast, have boat launches. Seabeck Marina also has a gas dock and moorage. Pleasant Harbor, to the south, has overnight moorage, restrooms, showers, and a small store. The nearest air fills are available in Bremerton on the east side of the canal or to the south in Potlatch.

Sub-Sea Environment: Broadleaf kelp clings to the rocks atop the pinnacle, and marine life abounds down the sloping sides to a depth of about 70 fsw, where it begins to diminish as surface light is reduced. Colorful sea stars, feather duster tube worms, hermit crabs, kelp crabs, decorator crabs, and white and orange plumose anemones are plentiful on the upper areas of Sea Mount. Kelp greenlings scatter quickly as divers happen by. Rockfish and greenlings dwell near the rocky sub-strate, while schools of shiner perch and tube-snouts circle above the encrusted boulders. Orange sea cucumbers and giant sea cucumbers are also bountiful on the reef, adding color to the gray backdrop. Larger fish include ling cod and cabezons. Red rock crabs, Dungeness crabs, and other shellfish at this site occasionally draw a wolf eel or a giant octopus onto the reef at feeding time. A scenic safety stop in the variegated kelp beds at the end of your dive reveals a myriad of kelp dwellers including blackeye gobies and frilly nudibranchs.

Sea Life:

Black sea bass
Blackeye gobies
Broadleaf kelp
Cabezons
Copper rockfish
Decorator crabs
Dungeness crabs
Feather duster tube worms
Giant octopuses
Giant sea cucumbers
Gunnels
Hermit crabs
Kelp crabs
Kelp greenlings

Ling cod
Nudibranchs
Orange plumose anemones
Orange sea cucumbers
Painted greenlings
Quillback rockfish
Red rock crabs
Sea stars
Shiner perch
Striped perch
Tube-snouts
White plumose anemones
Wolf eels

Seal Rock
• H O O D   C A N A L •

Dive Type: Natural rock reef
Location: North Hood Canal, Dabob Bay
Coordinates:
Dive Site: 47-42-97 N
122-53-07 W
Scenic Beach Boat Ramp: 47-39-30 N
122-50-15 W
Seabeck Marina: 47-38-55 N
122-49-75 W
Degree of Difficulty: All divers
Tricky Stuff: Approach, anchorage

Overview: Seal Rock is perfect site for a second or third dive in northern Hood Canal after an earlier deep dive at one of the Pulali Point sites (Dives #49 and #50) or at Sea Mount (Dive #51). It's also a good choice for an evening or night dive in this area. The busy reef is shallow and long bottom times are easily obtainable on a well-planned dive. Currents are minimal and marine life is plentiful.

The Dive in Depth: Approaching Seal Rock by boat and anchoring too close to the submerged but shallow portions of the rock are probably the biggest hazards visitors will encounter at this site. The bottom is solid, so drop down the anchor line on descent to check out the hold of the anchor before swimming off. Boat traffic usually pays heed to the big DANGER sign, reducing the threat of your getting propeller-whacked. Still, the sign may have been put there by someone who had already tried to drive a boat over the reef, so decorate your boat with a

This DANGER sign
marks the Seal Rock reef.
clearly visible dive flag. Current is nil, depth is not a consideration, and shore is nearby to the west, so even poor underwater navigators should be able to avoid getting lost. This is a mellow dive; enjoy!

Location: Seal Rock is located near shore in Dabob Bay (northern Hood Canal), about halfway between Wawa Point and the Dosewallips navigational buoy (see chart on page 165). Divers seeking a second dive site after a tour at Sea Mount or Pulali Point will easily find Seal Rock by watching for the DANGER sign along the shoreline as they travel south. Watch your depth sounder and anchor out from the sign in at least 25 fsw. A boat ramp nearby inside Wawa Point is usable at high tide, but a better one is to the north at Point Whitney. Scenic Beach State Park has a good ramp, and Seabeck Marina has a boat sling capable of launching boats up to 20 feet in length. Both of these launch sites are across Hood Canal to the southeast. Seabeck Marina also has a gas dock. Pleasant Harbor, about 2 miles south of the Dosewallips navigational buoy, has overnight moorage, restrooms, showers, and a small store. The nearest air fill stations are at Bremerton on the east side of the canal or at Potlatch to the south.

Sub-Sea Environment: Seal Rock pokes its gnarly noodle up out of the water even at high tide. This natural reef is composed of rough, glacier-hewn bedrock and broken-off rocks and boulders. Although eons of tidal exchanges have smoothed its edges, the subtidal terrain remains rugged and replete with crevices, cavities, and chasms, which serve as dens, dwellings, and domains for its denizens. Crabs and shrimp take shelter in the holes and hollows. Small schooling fish—shiner perch, striped perch, pile perch, and tube-snouts—move as a single unit and then scatter in front of divers. Greenlings and blackeye gobies add to the fish population of the reef. Color is provided by sea stars, sea cucumbers, and fragile, translucent nudibranchs. Even though the reef is fairly shallow (15–40 fsw) and well illuminated by penetrating sunlight, you may want to carry a dive light to search the gaps around the rocks and boulders.

Sea Life:

Decorator crabs
Giant sea cucumbers
Hermit crabs
Kelp greenlings
Kelp crabs
Nudibranchs
Orange sea cucumbers
Painted greenlings

Pile perch
Red rock crabs
Sea stars
Shiner perch
Shrimp
Striped perch
Tube-snouts

Misery Point Reef
• HOOD CANAL •

Dive Type: Artificial reef, concrete
Location: North Hood Canal, Seabeck area
Coordinates:
Dive Site: 47-39-42 N
122-49-97 W
Seabeck Marina: 47-38-55 N
122-49-75 W
Degree of Difficulty: All divers
Tricky Stuff: Boat traffic

Overview: This is one of several fishing reefs established over the years by the state of Washington. Immense concrete pillars and massive concrete slabs were dumped off barges in an effort to create habitat for bottom fish and thus enhance their populations. Because reefs populate more quickly in high-current areas and Hood Canal has very low currents, some of the other artificial reefs in the Sound have heavier populations of marine plants and animals. Still, this is an entertaining dive site and should not be overlooked. Time and experience have proven that when habitat is provided in Puget Sound, a reef begins to grow. This one has begun to grow as well, and diving here once a year will give you the chance to watch its ongoing development.

The Dive in Depth: Fishing boats have discarded some line and lures here—not necessarily on purpose—and small-boat traffic should be expected. In addition, Seabeck Marina is just inside the harbor to the east, and boaters frequently cut the corner over the top of this reef as they enter and exit. Always display a clearly visible diver-down flag. As in much of Hood Canal, currents are not strong at this site, but divers should nevertheless plan dives for slack current, especially if the boat is to be left unattended. The reef does drop from 40 to 100 feet, so plan your dive profile according to your comfort and experience level and monitor depth closely. Include a 15-foot safety stop in your dive plan.

Location: This fishing reef is located in Hood Canal, just south of the mouth of Seabeck Bay, 600 feet north of the Misery Point navigational light. A red-and-white State of Washington Department of Fisheries fishing reef buoy currently bobs above the slabs and pillars. The bottom surrounding the reef is primarily sand, and anchorage is good. Scenic Beach State Park just to the south has a nice ramp, and Seabeck Marina to the east has a sling for launching boats up to 20 feet in length. Seabeck Marina also has short- and long-term moorage and a fuel dock. The closest air fills are in Bremerton, about 15 miles east of Seabeck.

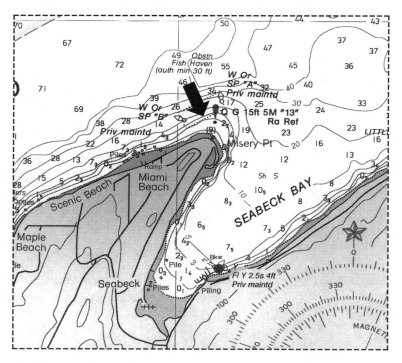

Sub-Sea Environment: Hood Canal has a substantial population of ling cod and cabezons, and they have already begun to frequent this reef for the free lunch that awaits on the aggregate substrate. The long, hollow pillars are perfect retreats for ling cod—in fact, the entire reef looks like a ling cod hotel, and the number of tenants is rapidly increasing. Quillback rockfish, striped perch, and shiner perch have taken up residence here, and an occasional sculpin or ratfish is no longer an unusual sight. White plumose anemones and giant sea cucumbers, together with sunflower stars, mottled stars, and sun stars, lighten and brighten the gloomy, gray concrete. Flounders blend in on the sandy bottom, sharing the area with a good variety of invertebrates. On an overcast day this dive becomes almost eerie, looking more like a dark, silent moonscape than a living reef. Still, it's well worth a tank of air.

Sea Life:

Cabezons	*Quillback rockfish*
Flounders	*Ratfish*
Giant sea cucumbers	*Sculpins*
Jellyfish	*Sea pens*
Kelp	*Shiner perch*
Ling cod	*Snails*
Moon snails	*Striped perch*
Mottled stars	*Sun stars*
Nudibranchs	*Sunflower stars*
Orange cucumbers	*White plumose anemones*

DIVE

SITE

Quatsap Point
• HOOD CANAL •

Dive Type: Natural rock reef
Location: North Hood Canal, south of Pleasant Harbor
Coordinates:
Dive Site: 47-39-67 N
122-54-08 W
Scenic Beach Ramp: 47-39-30 N
122-50-15 W
Seabeck Marina: 47-38-55 N
122-49-75 W
Degree of Difficulty: All divers
Tricky Stuff: None

Shoreline *at Quatsap Point.*

174

Overview: Because this is a fairly shallow reef, penetrating sunlight brightens the entire area. You'll be treated to a stunningly beautiful dive site, brilliant with color and teeming with graceful sea creatures. Divers seeking an overnight adventure should consider an excursion to this upper area of Hood Canal. Several good dive sites are nearby, and Pleasant Harbor, just to the north, has overnight moorage available with a store, restrooms, and showers. Perhaps such an adventure could be enhanced with a night dive at this site near the marina. Quatsap Point is also a natural fit as a second dive into plans involving a deep first dive at the Sea Mount (Dive #51) or one of the Pulali Point dive sites (Dives #49 and #50).

The Dive in Depth: This site is suitable for all levels of divers. The reef is shallow, and current is negligible. However, winds can be substantial on Hood Canal, and divers should verify a good set of the anchor before swimming away from an untended boat. As always, fly a flag.

Location: Quatsap Point is located just to the south of Pleasant Harbor in northern Hood Canal. Pleasant Harbor is protected on its southern and eastern sides by a peninsula, and this dive site is off the protruding rock bluff at the southeastern corner of this peninsula. Drop anchor near shore in 20–25 fsw and swim out to the wall. Boat launches are to the north at Whitney Point and Wawa Point, and Triton Cove has a nice ramp and dock to the south. The closest launch is across Hood Canal at Scenic Beach. Seabeck Marina has a boat sling and can launch boats up to 20 feet in length. Seabeck also has a gas dock. Divers launching from the east side can get air tanks filled in Bremerton. On the west side, the nearest air fills are at Potlatch, south of Hoodsport.

Sub-Sea Environment: Quatsap Point boasts a variegated wall that runs from 20 to 45 fsw and an aggregation of rock and boulders that provide the substrate for the living reef. Among the medley of fish gleaming in the penetrating sunlight between surface and the encrusted rocks are dense schools of glittering tube-snouts, pile perch, striped perch, and shiner perch. Broadleaf kelp blankets the rocky reeftop, casting its gorgeous hues of reds, browns, and greens into the backdrop of this seascape, while delicate spider crabs and nudibranchs shelter in its folds. Descending farther down the reef, divers are likely to encounter copper rockfish, quillback rockfish, kelp greenlings, and ling cod. Plumose anemones live in gigantic communities or in solitary unconfinement where they lend a ghostly ambience to a gloomy boulder. Strawberry anemones, feather duster tube worms,

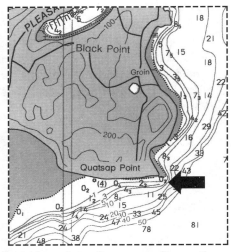

sea cucumbers, chitons, and a wide variety of sea stars all contribute beauty and diversity to the Quatsap Point reef.

Sea Life:

Broadleaf kelp	Plumose anemones
Chitons	Quillback rockfish
Copper rockfish	Sea stars
Feather duster tube worms	Sea cucumbers
Gobies	Shiner perch
Gunnels	Shrimp
Kelp crabs	Snails
Kelp greenlings	Spider crabs
Ling cod	Strawberry anemones
Nudibranchs	Striped perch
Pile perch	Tube-snouts

← →

Rosie's Ravine and Goby Garden
• HOOD CANAL •

Dive Type: Wall dive
Location: Central Hood Canal, McDaniel Cove,
  south of Pleasant Harbor
Coordinates:
  Dive Site: 47-37-97 N
  122-56-46 W
  Triton Cove Boat Launch: 47-36-51 N
  122-58-98 W
  Seabeck Marina: 47-38-55 N
  122-49-75 W
Degree of Difficulty: All divers to advanced divers,
  depending on depth
Tricky Stuff: Depth

This bluff, with the fence on top, is the landmark for Rosie's Ravine and Goby Garden.

Overview: This dive site is a twofer. It offers a deep, winding ravine wall for divers to inspect during a morning visit to the reef, and shallow walls and ledges brimming with marine life for a less demanding return trip after lunch when nitrogen levels have dropped. A sand-and-cobblestone bottom at both ends of the site brings variety to the seascape and supports a further diversity of creatures.

The Dive in Depth: Although Rosie's Ravine is an advanced dive because of depth, the Goby Garden portions of this site are suitable for all levels of divers. Currents are weak and variable, and diving from an anchored boat is no problem. Deep divers should plan for a 3-minute safety stop in 15-foot shallows.

Location: Rosie's Ravine and Goby Garden are located just north of McDaniel Cove in central Hood Canal. An obvious rock bluff juts out into the Canal about one-half mile north of McDaniel Cove. Anchor at the north end of the bluff in 20–30 fsw, slide down the anchor line, and swim out to the east to find the deep wall. Goby Garden is the area of small walls in 35–50 fsw that run parallel to the surface bluff. Patches of sand and cobblestones separate the gardens. One good boat launch with

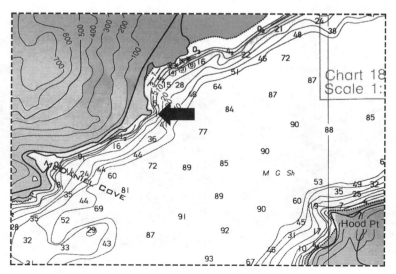

a dock is nearby at Triton Cove to the south; another nice launch is across the Canal and farther north, at Scenic Beach State Park. A boat sling at Seabeck Marina launches boats up to 20 feet in length. Nearest air fills can be obtained to the south at Potlatch or in Bremerton, about 15 miles east of Seabeck.

Sub-Sea Environment: Even the top of the deep wall at Rosie's Ravine is deep, at 75 fsw, and the wall drops precipitously to 130 fsw. The meandering, silt-covered wall reveals many cracks and crevasses where rockfish, octopuses, and black sea bass seek shelter during their non-feeding hours. Crabs and striped perch also make periodic visits to the deeper reaches of the reef. The shallower walls at 35–50 fsw, which comprise Goby Garden, are more colorful and more densely populated with sea life. Large communities of both orange and white plumose anemones extend their tentacles into the brine to capture planktonic animals. Elegant anemones, small metridium anemones, tube worms, sea staghorns, and sponges brighten the gray substrate and create shelter for shrimp and other small reef dwellers. Broadleaf kelp is abundant in patches at this site and, of course, blackeye gobies are thicker than ants at a picnic. You're also likely to see a range of additional creatures, from Dungeness crabs to gumboot chitons.

Sea Life:

Black sea bass
Blackeye gobies
Broadleaf kelp
Crabs
Dungeness crabs
Elegant anemones
Gumboot chitons
Hermit crabs
Kelp greenlings
Ling cod
Metridium anemones
Nudibranchs
Octopuses

Orange plumose anemones
Painted greenlings
Red rock crabs
Rockfish
Sea cucumbers
Sea staghorns
Shiner perch
Shrimp
Spider crabs
Sponges
Striped perch
Tube worms

Triton Cove
• HOOD CANAL •

Dive Type: Natural rock reef
Location: Central Hood Canal, north of Eldon
Coordinates:
Dive Site: 47-36-36 N
122-58-77 W
Triton Cove Boat Launch: 47-36-51 N
122-58-98 W
Seabeck Marina: 47-38-55 N
122-49-75 W
Scenic Beach Ramp: 47-39-30 N
122-50-15 W
Degree of Difficulty: All divers
Tricky Stuff: Anchorage

Overview: At high tide the rocky reef at the south point of Triton Cove is an island; at low tide, it's a peninsula. The reef pyramids down to 75 feet, creating a vast diveable area. You'll need several repeat visits to explore the entire site and discover the full spectrum of plants and animals residing in Triton Cove. This site has all the beauty we've come to expect on natural rock reefs in the Northwest. Its lack of currents, combined with its interesting and colorful marine life, make it an exquisite location for underwater photography.

The Dive in Depth: This is a great dive for all levels of divers! A few small boats maneuver in and out of the cove, but the wise ones give a wide berth to the treacherous rocks. Still, it can be difficult to tell which ones are the wise ones, so clearly display a diver-down flag on your boat

The dive site is east of these rocks at Triton Cove.

and swim up the rocks to the shallows at the end of your dive. Watch for discarded fishing line. Currents in this portion of Hood Canal are inconsequential and therefore easy to swim against. The substrate is rocky, so descend on the anchor line and check the set of the anchor, just in case winds should come up and try to relocate your untended boat.

Location: Triton Cove is located on the west side of Hood Canal, about halfway between Eldon and Pleasant Harbor. The boat launch at Triton Cove is one of the nicest on Hood Canal, and it has a dock. The dive site is on the south tip of the cove opening, a short distance from the ramp. For those who want to launch on the east side of the Canal, a boat sling at Seabeck Marina launches boats up to 20 feet in length, and a good ramp is available just to the south of Seabeck at Scenic Beach. Divers out for a two-tank day can choose any of three other nearby dive sites as a first or second dive; the reef north of the pilings at the Jorstad Creek area (Dive #57), Rosie's Ravine to the north (Dive #55), or the Quatsap Point Dive (#54) yet farther to the north. The nearest air fills are at either of two scuba shops at the town of Potlatch, south of Hoodsport.

Sub-Sea Environment: This natural reef consists of massive bedrock, a scatter of broken rocks and boulders, a series of small walls

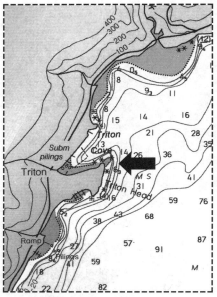

and ledges, and solid rock spines that eventually give way to a sandy bottom. Colorful sponges and corals are accented by vibrant, multicolored sea stars, orange cucumbers, and white and orange plumose anemones. Large schools of striped perch and shiner perch add a surreal touch to the variegated backdrop of the brightly painted reef. Blackeye gobies poke their blunt little noses from seemingly every nook and cranny, occasionally getting inadvertently caught up in a game of aquatic dodge ball as fleeing crabs scamper sideways to elude passing divers. Rockfish and quillbacks repose on the ledges and are accompanied on the reef by ling cod and cabezons. Other denizens here include greenlings, flounders, hermit crabs, and giant sea cucumbers. Numerous seaweeds and kelps grow on the Triton Cove reef, giving the dive site an aquarium-like atmosphere.

Sea Life:

Blackeye gobies	*Orange cucumbers*
Brown rockfish	*Orange plumose anemones*
Cabezons	*Painted greenlings*
Copper rockfish	*Quillback rockfish*
Corals	*Sea stars*
Flounders	*Seaweeds*
Giant sea cucumbers	*Shiner perch*
Hermit crabs	*Spider crabs*
Kelp greenlings	*Sponges*
Kelps	*Striped perch*
Ling cod	*White plumose anemones*

Jorstad Creek Area
• H O O D   C A N A L •

Dive Type: Natural rock reef with walls
Location: Central Hood Canal, south of Eldon
Coordinates:
  Dive Site: 47-31-93 N
  122-02-53 W
  Seabeck Marina: 47-38-55 N
  122-49-75 W
  Scenic Beach: 47-39-30 N
  122-50-15   W
  Tacoma City Light Boat Ramp: 47-22-12 N
  123-09-43 W
Degree of Difficulty: All divers
Tricky Stuff: None

Overview: The Jorstad Creek area of Hood Canal offers divers a multiplicity of sites to explore. Shallow walls, deep walls, and bedrock ribs compose the seascape and offer habitat that is as varied as its inhabitants. This site is easy to find and, although we describe a specific portion of the area here, all of the bottom structure along the bluff is rewarding territory. Although most of us have to travel a long way to reach this site, it offers the convenience of a full day of diving on substantial and varied terrain.

The Dive in Depth: This site has something to offer all levels of scuba divers. Depth is the main hazard here, but the way the rock ledges out to 65 feet before dropping down on the deep wall allows less-experienced divers to tour the larger, more colorful upper reaches of the reef.

Advanced divers can explore the deep wall before ascending to an interesting safety stop along the top of the reef. Boat traffic is a potential hazard to divers, as it is anywhere. Currents are minimal in this part of Hood Canal.

Location: This dive site is located near Jorstad Creek, south of the town of Eldon, on Hood Canal. Dozens of pilings are clearly visible along the shoreline, and the deep wall is about 200 yards north of the northernmost piling. North of the pilings is a small sandy beach, and north of the sandy beach a rock bluff is obvious on the shoreline; the deep wall is straight out to the east of this bluff. The two shallower walls can be found in 30–50 fsw just to the south of the deep wall, and south of these shallower walls is a bedrock rib that runs from shallow to 50 fsw. Although divers can easily visit all of these attractions on one tank of air, a close inspection of the site requires several visits. Additionally, the area to the north of the deep wall offers elaborate sub-sea structures and is well worth a repeat trip to the site. Boat launches are at Scenic Beach State Park south of Seabeck and Seabeck Marina on the east side of the Canal. On the west side of the Canal, launch at Mike's Beach Resort near milepost 318 on US Highway 101. Another good ramp is to the north at Triton Cove, which also has a dock. Air fills can be obtained at either of two dive shops in Potlatch, where there is also a free boat launch provided by Tacoma City Light. For those launching on the east side, air fills are in Bremerton, about 15 miles east of Seabeck.

Sub-Sea Environment: Not far from shore, a layer of gray silt blankets a deep wall that drops from 65 fsw to 120 fsw. Cracks and crevasses along the wall make perfect dens for octopuses and wolf eels. Some large fish, including ling cod, black sea bass, and kelp greenlings, live on the reef, but the commonest species here are striped perch, shiner perch, pile perch, tube-snouts, and several species of rockfish. Shallow walls from 30 to 50 fsw, just south of the deep wall, are painted with a rainbow of invertebrates, including sea cucumbers and sea stars. Patches of broadleaf kelp decorate the reef with hues of green and brown and give refuge to kelp crabs, decorator crabs, painted greenlings, and blackeye gobies. Farther south, a solid rock rib, sheathed with white plumose

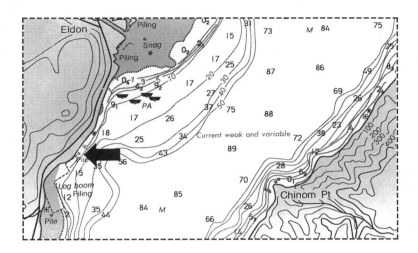

anemones, is attended by huge schools of baitfish and platoons of crabs. Ascending from the deep wall to the shallower portions of the reef lets divers discharge a little excess nitrogen while they inspect the more colorful marine plants and animals highlighted by the penetrating sunlight.

Sea Life:

Black sea bass	Painted greenlings
Blackeye gobies	Pile perch
Broadleaf kelp	Red rock crabs
Decorator crabs	Rockfish
Dungeness crabs	Shiner perch
Giant sea cucumbers	Snails
Kelp crabs	Striped perch
Kelp greenlings	Sun stars
Leather stars	Sunflower stars
Ling cod	Tube-snouts
Octopuses	White plumose anemones
Orange sea cucumbers	Wolf eels

DIVE

58

SITE

Whip Garden
• HOOD CANAL •

Dive Type: Natural rock reef
Location: South Hood Canal, south of Dewatto Bay
Coordinates:
   Dive Site: 47-26-68 N
   123-05-09 W
   Tacoma City Light Boat Ramp: 47-22-12 N
   123-09-43 W
   Hoodsport Marina: 47-24-20 N
   123-08-40 W
Degree of Difficulty: Intermediate
Tricky Stuff: Anchorage

Overview: Each dive site has something different to offer. This uniqueness is part of what fills us with wonder as we behold the undersea world and scrutinize the varied marine life we are privileged to witness. Finding a few sea whips, majestic members of the Cnidarian family, is always a delightful experience for Hood Canal divers. At Whip Garden, in this tiny cove south of Dewatto Bay, you can cruise through hundreds of these creatures and enjoy a truly captivating experience.

The Dive in Depth: Although a difficulty rating on this dive would otherwise be very low, Whip Garden is deep, so the site should be considered intermediate to advanced. The sandy bottom at this site drops off so fast that anchorage can be difficult in even the slightest wind. If any wind is blowing to the north, anchor south of the point, descend on the anchor line to ensure a good bite, and begin your dive to the north—or consider using a live boat scenario. Currents are minimal in this area of Hood Canal.

186

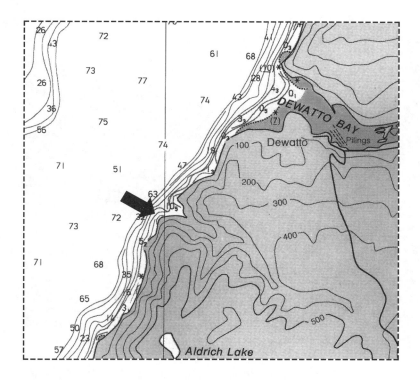

Location: This dive site is located on the southern tip of the small cove just to the south of Dewatto Bay in Hood Canal. A small house (currently white) sits at the back of the cove. The cove side of the dive site runs east–west, while the Canal side of the site runs north–south. Both shorelines drop off rapidly to well beyond recreational diving limits, with the Canal side offering the better anchorage if the wind is blowing to the north. Boat launches are the Tacoma City Light Ramp at Potlatch and a boat sling at the Rest-a-While Resort in Hoodsport. Overnight moorage is available at the Hoodsport Marina. Air fills are available from either of the two dive shops near Potlatch.

Sub-Sea Environment: Dungeness crabs, red rock crabs, and oodles of shrimp scurry across the sand-and-cobblestone substrate, where a variety of anemones and sea stars also reside. South of the southern

This small house *is sheltered inside the cove south of Dewatto Bay.*

point of this modest cove are a series of small walls at depths of 20–50 fsw. Quillback rockfish inhabit the walls, taking cover in the many crab-carved openings along the ledges. Blennies, painted greenlings, kelp greenlings, and ling cod live on the reef, joined by striped perch and schools of shiner perch. Many of the larger cobblestones serve as foundations for both white and orange plumose anemones. Flounders camouflage themselves in the silty sand. The most fascinating part of this dive, however, lies at depths between 70 and 90 fsw, where a virtual garden of sea whips encompasses the entire site in a dense belt from 20 to 30 feet wide. The pure white whips, 3 to 4 feet in height and majestic in appearance, seem to stand guard around the reef. Broadleaf kelp abounds along the tops of the walls and provides shelter for myriad small animals including snails, nudibranchs, and spider crabs. These kelp beds offer an intriguing area to explore while you are reducing your nitrogen level in the shallower waters.

A red rock *crab picnics on tube worms.*

Sea Life:

Anemones
Blennies
Broadleaf kelp
Dungeness crabs
Flounders
Kelp greenlings
Ling cod
Nudibranchs
Orange plumose anemones
Painted greenlings

Quillback rockfish
Red rock crabs
Sea stars
Shiner perch
Shrimp
Snails
Spider crabs
Striped perch
White plumose anemones

DIVE
59
SITE

Sund Rock North Wall
• HOOD CANAL •

Dive Type: Natural rock reef
Location: Central Hood Canal, south of Lilliwaup
Coordinates:
   Dive Site: 47-26-14 N
   123-07-22 W
   Tacoma City Light Boat Ramp: 47-22-12 N
   123-09-43 W
   Hoodsport Marina: 47-24-20 N
   123-08-40 W
Degree of Difficulty: All divers
Tricky Stuff: None

Overview: "Look but don't take" is the mandatory procedure at this marine preserve in central Hood Canal. Stiff fines can be levied against divers who take anything at all from this site. Large marine creatures are common on the North Wall, and current is negligible. A two-tank trip that includes Sund Rock (Dive #60) and the North Wall constitutes an unforgettable day of diving in Hood Canal.

The Dive in Depth: This is a good site for all levels of scuba divers. Current during exchanges is easy to swim against, and the reef offers plenty of visuals from the top to the maximum depth of about 75 fsw. There are fish pens to the south of the reef that divers should avoid, but they are far enough from the dive site to be of little threat to anyone except the very worst of navigators. If you have left the reef and are unable to relocate it, swim west to shallow water, look up and reach up during your ascent, and all should be well. Winds are common in Hood

Canal, and boat divers should always descend on the anchor line to ensure a good firm set of the anchor when leaving an untended boat at the surface.

Location: Although it is called the North Wall of Sund Rock, this site is some distance from Sund Rock (Dive #60). Fish pens, easily visible from a boat, lie between the two sites and are the most obvious point of reference when you arrive in the area. To find the North Wall, locate the triangular-shaped Sund Rock bluff south of the pens and begin to navigate slowly to the north. About 200 yards north of the Sund Rock, another rock bluff is evident on shore. At the far northern end of that bluff, you will see trees along the

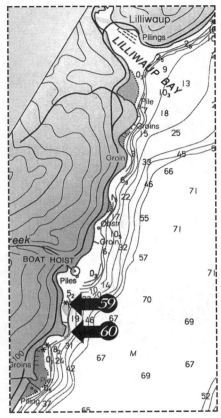

waterline that give way, again to the north, to what appears to be a dry creek bed. The North Wall lies to the east of the creek bed in 15–75 fsw. Boat launches are at the Tacoma City Light Boat Ramp at Potlatch, the Rest-a-While Resort at Hoodsport, and Mike's Beach Resort near milepost 318 north of Hoodsport. Air fills can be obtained from two dive shops near Potlatch. The Hoodsport launch site also has a fuel dock. Hoodsport Marina offers overnight moorage. Air fills can be obtained from two dives shops near Potlatch.

Sub-Sea Environment: A solid bedrock rib running east-west and the south side of that rib, which is composed of boulders and broken

The fish pens *near the North Wall of Sund Rock.*

rock, make up this prolific reef. White and orange plumose anemones appear luminous as they reflect penetrating sunlight and help brighten the silt-coated rocks. Broken shells littering the bottom bear witness to the hungry wolf eels and octopuses that live and feed on the reef. Ling cod, kelp greenlings, rockfish, and huge schools of shiner perch inhabit the rocky site. Flounders bury themselves on the silty bottom among anemones and hydroids, where they are joined by Dungeness and red rock crabs. The top of the rock rib is blanketed with broadleaf kelp. End your dive with a safety-stop tour of this colorful environment and the many small marine creatures it shelters.

Sea Life:

Blackeye gobies
Broadleaf kelp
China rockfish
Clams
Dungeness crabs
Flounders
Frosted nudibranchs
Hydroids
Kelp greenlings
Ling cod
Orange plumose anemones

Painted greenlings
Quillback rockfish
Red rock crabs
Scallops
Sea bass
Shiner perch
Shrimp
Striped perch
Tube worms
White plumose anemones

Sund Rock

• H O O D   C A N A L •

Dive Type: Natural rock reef
Location: Central Hood Canal, south of Lilliwaup
Coordinates:
   Dive Site: 47-26-15 N
   123-07-18 W
   Tacoma City Light Boat Ramp: 47-22-12 N
   123-09-43 W
Degree of Difficulty: All divers
Tricky Stuff: Anchorage

Overview: This marine preserve offers a beautiful dive on a natural rock wall that slopes gradually to a sandy bottom. Once renowned as a shore dive until local property owners grew weary of improper behavior by certain visitors, this site should now be considered for boat diving only. Viewing a reef this densely populated with marine life provides divers with a standard of comparison for other Hood Canal dive sites and perhaps raises their awareness of the ongoing depletion of our underwater world. Many sites that once virtually gleamed like crown jewels against a silt-coated backdrop now appear nearly barren from human thoughtlessness and greed when compared to the splendor of Sund Rock. Bring your camera, watch your fin kicks, take only pictures, and leave only bubbles.

The Dive in Depth: This dive is recommended for all levels of scuba divers who are comfortable with boat diving and have learned buoyancy control. Currents in this part of Hood Canal are weak and easy to swim against. The depth at the bottom of this reef is about 80 feet, but new

The shoreline *at Sund Rock.*

divers have no need to venture that deep to find the octopuses or other marine creatures living on the reef. This site is heavily populated with sea life from the surface to the bottom, and all divers will have plenty to see at their preferred depth range. Sund Rock provides poor anchorage, so anchor on the sandy bottom of the small cove to the north of the rock. Boat traffic is not typically heavy at Sund Rock, but, as always, ascending up the rock wall at the completion of your dive, while looking up and reaching up, is good basic procedure. Fly a dive flag, watch your bottom time, make a safety stop, and enjoy! There are fish pens to the north, but they are far enough from the site to not become a hazard to divers visiting Sund Rock.

Location: Sund Rock is located on the west side of central Hood Canal about halfway between Hoodsport and Lilliwaup (see chart on page 191). Although houses perched on the southern exposure of a triangular rock bluff are one indicator of the site location, the best landmark is the

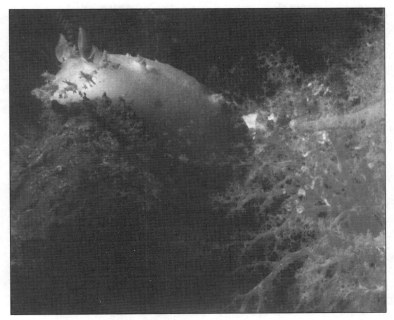

Clown nudibranch *and orange cucumber.*

fish pens to the immediate north of the site. The reef is located below the rock bluff to the south of the fish pens. To avoid damaging the reef, anchor just north of the site, west of the fish pens, in the small cove and swim over to the reef. The cove also helps provide protection against winds which, when strong enough, can cause anchors to pull free. Please remember that nothing may be taken from the site and that the shoreline and tideland are privately owned. Anchor in at least 20 fsw and respect the rights of the families who live and raise their children here. There is a free boat launch with restrooms, a telephone, a picnic area, and plenty of free parking at the Tacoma City Light Boat launch in Potlatch, south of the site. Air fills are also available in Potlatch.

Sub-Sea Environment: Octopuses and wolf eels make their dens in the cracks and fissures along the walls of Sund Rock and lend their always-engrossing presence to the enchantment divers find on this reef.

Quillback rockfish, kelp greenlings, and ling cod are plentiful, accompanied by tube-snouts and schools of perch. In fact, all of the aquatic creatures once so abundant in Hood Canal are still numerous at this protected site, and they seem both curious and comfortable when divers join them for a tour of their neighborhood. Colorful sea stars creep around on the rocks and ledges, and countless white plumose anemones cloak the tops of the escarpments. Sea cucumbers, corals, sponges, and tube worms lend their brilliant colors to an undersea canvas rich with life and movement. Alabaster and clown nudibranchs, chitons, sea squirts, and sea whips dwell on the reef at Sund Rock, as do red rock and Dungeness crabs. In the shallows, decorator crabs and kelp crabs rule their domain over the smaller creatures who find comfort within the shelter of the kelp.

Sea Life:

Alabaster nudibranchs
China rockfish
Chitons
Clams
Clown nudibranchs
Corals
Decorator crabs
Dungeness crabs
Flounders
Giant sea cucumbers
Hermit crabs
Kelp
Kelp crabs
Kelp greenlings
Limpets
Ling cod
Octopuses

Orange sea cucumbers
Pile perch
Quillback rockfish
Red rock crabs
Scallops
Sea squirts
Sea whips
Shiner perch
Snails
Sponges
Striped perch
Tube worms
Tube-snouts
White plumose anemones
White sea cucumbers
Wolf eels

Painted Greenling

Appendix 4

Hints for Better Divivng

■ Pick up a hose clip at your local scuba shop and attach it to the front of your BCD to hold your gauges in front of you and up off the reef. Your gauges will be easier to find and less likely to get tangled when you're diving on sunken boats and barges.

■ When drift diving, have the buddy team take along a 3-foot length of rope with a knot in each end for each diver to hold. Buddy separation is virtually eliminated, buddy contact is excellent, and divers are not continually looking around to see where their buddy is, so they can relax and enjoy the drift. Never attach ropes to divers or their equipment!

■ Buddy teams should always review hand signals before beginning their dives and agree on what minimum level of air pressure by either buddy will determine the start of their ascent.

■ When planning dives in high-current areas, arrive an hour ahead of calculated correct slack current, suit up, and watch the current go slack before starting your dive. Current tables, unfortunately, are not perfect, but dive planning for high-current areas must be.

■ If divers are struggling to get back into an anchored boat after the current has started to run, and the boat is tended, have the tender pull the anchor free. The boat and divers will then drift at nearly the same speed, allowing an easy entry back on board.

■ When boat diving, make sure everyone on board knows how to start and operate the boat. Making this a simple habit may someday eliminate a disaster.

■ When boat diving, a two-tub system works well. Have a poly tub for each buddy team for storing their gear in. This helps prevent masks, snorkels, knives, lights, gloves, etc. from getting lost, broken, or mixed up with others' equipment. When a team is in the water, their tub is empty; when they come back aboard, all their gear goes back in the tub. This also saves boat space by allowing divers to leave big equipment bags on shore.

■ On most dives, the best plan is to buddy up at the anchor line and descend on the line to inspect the set of the anchor. The perfect set is one that will hold the boat firmly, yet come free when pulled straight up. In current or windy conditions, drive the boat forward into the anchor line while someone takes up the slack. Do not attempt to free the anchor until the boat is directly over it. If diving at slack before flood, make sure adequate anchor line is available to allow for the rising water level.

■ On a small boat, dropping the anchor line into a bucket as it is pulled up will help prevent tangles and knots in the rope. This not only makes it much easier to drop anchor, but also reduces water in the bilge and keeps the already-limited floor space free from additional mess.

■ Reducing the sensitivity of a fishfinder often makes it easier to locate the reef, since false signals are muffled and small rocks and large anemones will not show up as bottom contour.

■ A 50-foot floating line cast out the back of the boat offers a larger target for divers swimming back to the boat in surface current or wind waves. It also gives them a place to rest and catch their breath before starting the task of removing gear and climbing aboard.

■ An 8-foot nylon strap, available at most sporting goods stores, with the male end of a 1-inch quick release affixed every 15 inches, can be attached to one of the cleats and left floating outside the boat during dives. Upon returning to the boat, divers can inflate their BCDs and clip them to the strap for quick recovery after they are on board. Most BCDs are equipped with 1-inch quick releases on them somewhere. If they are not, it is easy to attach one of the female ends to them before divers enter the water. Carry a couple of extra female ends on short nylon web straps for future use.

Wolf eel

Epilogue

AUTHOR'S NOTE: *In the fall of 1995, I suffered excessive internal bleeding as a result of taking large doses of a popular painkiller that a dentist had prescribed. Within two weeks I had undergone 32 blood transfusions and two major surgeries. During that time, I survived three near-death situations. Since then, many people have asked me why I haven't written something about near-death experiences. The reason is that I have only a greater appreciation for life as a result of those times. "Goodnight, Today" was written in celebration of one day of my life after that fateful October. Now, at the end of each day, I feel that I could rewrite "Goodnight, Today"* . . . *to reflect the wonders I have been privileged to observe.*

Goodnight, Today

How pleased I am that we could be in the same place at the same time. Your shivering dawn brought goose bumps to my arms, and I could taste your frigid air chilling its path into my lungs so soon after your birth. As the sun rays collided with your adolescence to warm your early hours, I became overwhelmed by your pristine beauty and unassuming innocence.

To have met you on the beach seems such a wonder, having met so many yesterdays in other places, and the possibility of predestination of such a meeting is beyond my comprehension, leaving only chance to explain away that wonder. It was an honor to share the sound and smell of your foamy surf; others should be so lucky, though none were that I know of. You squished your wet, warm sand up between my toes as I marveled at your horizon for an unknown time before you sent the clouds for my consideration.

What excitement you instill in your animals! Seals barking for reasons only they know as the gulls wheel about in great circles, conspiring against their prey. Sandpipers scurrying east and west with the surf, seeming to discover that which most intrigues a sandpiper, while the sand shrimp flip and flop about having been booted out of bed by the surf. Miniature crabs furiously racing sideways from place to place, always on the lookout yet hopelessly defenseless against the hungry, screeching gulls.

You mussed my hair, Today, as you swept me along with your sand-filled breeze. You filled my eyes and ears and nose with your tiny grit while you were filling them with your phenomenal sights, curious sounds, and astonishing smells.

I watched in awe as you went your way, leaving me behind. My heart pounded, my throat clenched, and my eyes watered when I tried to say good-bye. You seemed not to notice or care as the darkness pursued you, but perhaps you will have memories of me as I surely will of you. As you have met my father's son, so I too hope to meet your offspring... may Tomorrow find me somewhere and share its pleasures as you have shared yours.

—D. Bliss
March 27, 1996

Index

Index